Editorial Project Manager
Lorin E. Klistoff, M.A.

Illustrator
Teacher Created Resources Staff

Cover Artist
Brenda DiAntonis

Managing Editor
Ina Massler Levin, M.A.

Creative Director
Karen J. Goldfluss, M.S. Ed.

Art Production Manager
Kevin Barnes

Art Coordinator
Renée Christine Yates

Imaging
James Edward Grace

Translation
Spanish language translation
provided by Translations.com

Publisher
Mary D. Smith, M.S. Ed.

Writing Effective Report Card Comments

Spanish and English Edition

- Easy-to-use format • Covers a variety of topics
- Clear, concise, and constructive comments

"He expresses his ideas clearly."

"Él expresa sus ideas claramente."

Authors

Kathy Dickinson Crane and Kathleen Law

Teacher Created Resources, Inc.
6421 Industry Way
Westminster, CA 92683
www.teachercreated.com

ISBN: 978-1-4206-8858-0

© *2007 Teacher Created Resources, Inc.*
Reprinted, 2011
Made in U.S.A.

Teacher Created Resources

Table of Contents

Introduction

A report card is a keepsake that many students will treasure their entire lives! With this thought in mind, the comments a teacher writes on a report card become vital. Report card comments should not only be clear, concise, and constructive, they must also be positive, personal, and powerful.

Report card comments will have an impact on parents, as well as students, so they must be thoughtfully written. A poorly written comment may upset or confuse parents. Instead of receiving parental support, you may cause a rift between the parents and the school or damage the relationship between parent and child. Rather than saying "John is failing math," you can choose comments from this book to state, "John is a fun-loving and happy boy, but he is struggling in math. He needs to work every night, beginning with the multiplication facts through the fives. Please help him review these facts at home." With the comments in this book, you can always take a positive approach or suggest a possible solution. This will strengthen the connection with your student's parents and help you achieve your goal of improving student performance.

This book is organized in an easy-to-use format. It is divided into specific areas that generally need reporting and benefit from clarification. A teacher should be able to turn to the table of contents to be directed to a specific section to find a ready-made comment. If a comment needs expansion or individualization, the Words and Phrases section should help stimulate thought to write the perfect comment with precision and thoughtfulness.

All comments have been translated into Spanish so both Spanish and English appear on the page. This is for the teacher who does not speak Spanish but wants to communicate with Spanish-speaking parents. It is a way to open the lines of communication between school and home so everyone is on the same page about student progress.

A teacher's well chosen words will be the exact complement needed to make the report card not only a keepsake, but a useful tool that will stimulate communication between the parent and the child, encourage extra practice, and/or provide parents with concrete, relevant examples of their child's performance and progress in school.

Assessment Methods

Why Assess?

From the moment a student enters the classroom, an effective teacher is observing, evaluating, and assessing. A teacher's ultimate desire is for each student to succeed and reach full potential while under his or her care.

Classroom assessments can be formal or informal, but whatever the method, the purpose for any assessment is to inform the teacher so he or she can tailor instruction to the needs of the individual and the group. Armed with this information, a teacher can give every student multiple opportunities for further practice and greater success.

Students are multifaceted! To gain greater insight, teachers should use a wide variety of assessment tools. This provides a broader base from which to collect information related to student success and the curriculum.

To optimize the benefit of assessments, parents can be brought in as partners by using effective reporting systems and communicating comments constructively. This communication should be ongoing, timely, clear, and meaningful.

Types of Assessments

The following lists different types of assessment:

- Individual Assessments: Both oral and written questions or formal testing methods

- Group Assessments: Focusing on the work of the whole group in a cooperative setting

- Anecdotal Notes or Records: Recording behaviors or specific incidents throughout the day

- Portfolios: A collection of student work showing growth during a specific time period

- Observational Checklist: Keeping track of skills mastered, strengths, and weaknesses

- Teacher/Student Conferences or Workshops: Meeting with students to discuss specific work, writings, etc.

- Projects: Assignments given to develop specific items, written reports, or creations that require independent action

- Inventories: A sampling of skills tested for diagnostic purposes

- Questioning: A variety of questions to evaluate the student's thinking and reasoning skills

Assessment Methods

Time To Assess

As a teacher begins to develop approaches for effective student evaluation, consideration must be given to scheduling time to plan, developing assessment instruments, collecting and analyzing data, reporting, and adapting teaching styles to reflect student learning.

Following are a few suggestions to lighten the load of assessment:

- *Collaborate with colleagues:* Sharing the task lightens the load.

- *Share evaluation tasks with students:* Create systems of peer tutoring or incorporate self-assessment procedures. Allow students to participate in record keeping.

- *Plan effective methods of storing data:* Keep organized. Use binders, spreadsheets, or computer programs to keep information in a central location.

- *Keep anecdotal records handy:* Place the record book in an accessible location. Consider using sticky notes or index cards to help with the management.

- *Train students to organize portfolios:* Students will benefit from instruction and gain practice in organizing and maintaining a portfolio.

- *Record observational checklists in a timely manner:* If a behavior or skill is observed, record it!

Build a Home-School Connection

The reporting of student assessments brings to the parents' attention areas of strengths or weaknesses in a child. Increased dialogue between home and school will create a partnership for student growth and motivation and increase academic success.

Academic Areas

The school day is filled with a myriad of subject matter. Some students are shining stars in all facets of the school day. Most students, however, tend to excel in some areas more than others. Unfortunately, some students struggle in multiple areas.

Whatever the circumstance of the student, progress needs to be reported. Many will have areas where improvement is needed, and specifics can be given to parents that will allow them to give extra help and support. For others, positive comments may just be the motivator for continued success.

This section is divided into academic categories. Choose an academic subject, and you will find comments tailored to fit your students' needs.

Handwriting

Proficient (Competente)

◆ _____ has great penmanship and takes pride in his/her work.

❖ _____ tiene muy buena letra y se toma sus tareas muy en serio.

◆ _____ has placed great effort in his/her handwriting. He/she is able to correctly form most of the letters.

❖ _____ se ha esforzado mucho para mejorar su letra. Ahora escribe correctamente la mayoría de las letras.

◆ It is a joy to read _____'s handwriting. He/she continues to put forth his/her best effort.

❖ Es un placer leer la letra de _____ . Se nota que sigue haciendo su mayor esfuerzo.

Making Progress (Está Progresando)

◆ _____ has made great effort to better his/her penmanship.

❖ _____ se ha esforzado mucho para mejorar su letra.

◆ With extra effort, _____'s handwriting will continue to improve. Please encourage him/her to practice at home.

❖ Con un poco más de esfuerzo, la letra de _____ mejorará aún más. Por favor motivenlo(a) para que practique en su casa.

◆ It is easy to tell that _____ is ready to improve his/her penmanship. He/she has shown great ability in following directions and seems to give the time necessary for correct letter formation.

❖ Se nota que _____ quiere mejorar su letra. Ha demostrado gran capacidad para seguir instrucciones y parece dedicar el tiempo necesario para correctamente formar su letra.

Handwriting

Needs Improvement (Necesita Mejorar)

◆ It is challenging to decipher _____'s written work. He/she needs to slow down and try to achieve his/her best handwriting with each assignment.

❖ Es difícil entender la letra de _____ . Necesita trabajar más lentamente y tratar de lograr su mejor escritura en cada tarea.

◆ _____ seems to find handwriting a challenge. He/she needs considerable practice in letter formation and directionality. I have enclosed a set of handwriting pages; please help _____ complete these at home.

❖ Aparentemente, a _____ le resulta difícil escribir las letras. Necesita practicar bastante el trazado de las letras y darles direccionalidad. Adjunte varias páginas para practicar la escritura. Por favor ayuden a _____ para que las completen en su casa.

◆ _____ needs to develop his/her fine motor skills. He/she will benefit from working with small manipulatives to strengthen hand muscles.

❖ _____ necesita desarrollar sus destrezas motoras finas. Se beneficiará si trabaja con pequeños objetos didácticos para fortalecer los músculos de la mano.

Listening

Proficient (Competente)

◆ _____ is very attentive and listens thoroughly in all settings.

❖ _____ pone mucha atención y escucha con gran interés en todas las situaciones.

◆ _____ enjoys listening to stories. It is a joy to read to him/her!

❖ A _____ le gusta escuchar relatos. ¡Es un placer leerle!

◆ _____ listens carefully and evaluates what he/she hears.

❖ _____ escucha con atención y evalúa lo que oye.

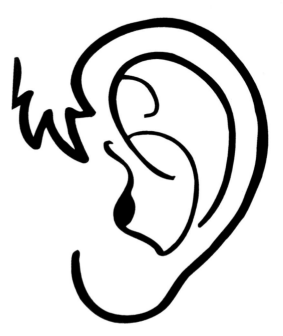

Making Progress (Está Progresando)

◆ _____ has improved in his/her listening. You can continue to increase his/her listening skills by making statements and giving one- or two-step directions that he/she then verbally repeats. This will help _____ focus on the spoken word.

❖ _____ ha mejorado mucho sus destrezas para escuchar. Usted puede ayudar a mejorarlas aún más si le pide que repita verbalmente oraciones e instrucciones de uno o dos pasos. Esto ayudará a que _____ se concentre en la palabra hablada.

◆ _____ is becoming a better listener. As a result, he/she is participating more in our discussions.

❖ _____ está mejorando sus destrezas para escuchar. En consecuencia, participa más en las discusiónes en clase.

◆ _____ has shown increased interest in his/her schoolwork because he/she has improved his/her listening skills.

❖ _____ ha demostrado mayor interés en sus tareas porque ha mejorado sus destrezas para escuchar.

Listening

Needs Improvement (Necesita Mejorar)

◆ _____ has a hard time listening. He/she may have an auditory problem; perhaps we should refer him/her for testing.

❖ _____ tiene dificultades para escuchar. Tal vez tenga algún problema auditivo y sea conveniente que le realicen pruebas auditivas.

◆ _____ has difficulty listening in class and is easily distracted by his/her classmates. He/she needs to listen and concentrate fully on the task at hand.

❖ _____ tiene dificultades para escuchar en clase y se distrae fácilmente con sus compañeros. Necesita escuchar y concentrarse por completo en la tarea que realiza.

◆ _____ does not always listen to instructions because his/her friends easily distract him/her. When he/she listens responsibly, _____ is able to put forth his/her best effort.

❖ _____ no siempre escucha las instrucciones porque sus compañeros lo/la distraen fácilmente. Cuando escucha con atención, _____ es capaz de poner su mejor esfuerzo.

Math

Proficient (Competente)

◆ _____ is highly proficient in math. I am challenging him/her.

❖ _____ es muy competente en matemáticas. Le estoy exigiendo según su capacidad.

◆ It is apparent that _____ enjoys math. He/she participates in class and can always explain his/her work.

❖ Es evidente que a _____ le gustan las matemáticas. Participa en clase y siempre puede explicar sus tareas.

◆ It is a joy to correct _____'s math work pages. He/she takes pride in his/her work and is very proficient in math.

❖ Es un placer corregir los trabajos de matemáticas de _____ . Se toma sus tareas muy en serio y es muy competente en la matemática.

◆ _____ can accurately construct and label a variety of graphs.

❖ _____ puede dibujar diferentes gráficas con precisión y ponerles nombres.

◆ _____ can create graphs and explain them to others.

❖ _____ puede dibujar gráficas y explicarlas.

◆ _____ can apply the knowledge of probability in sports, weather predictions, and games of chance.

❖ _____ puede aplicar el conocimiento de probabilidad en deportes, en el pronóstico del tiempo meteorológico y en juegos de azar.

◆ _____ uses appropriate mathematical language. He/she can communicate knowledge clearly and precisely.

❖ _____ usa lenguaje matemático apropiado. Puede comunicar sus conocimientos con claridad y precisión.

◆ _____ has a positive attitude towards math. He/she can demonstrate the process of addition and subtraction very easily.

❖ _____ tiene una actitud positiva hacia las matemáticas. Puede demostrar con gran facilidad el proceso de sumas y restas.

◆ _____ can easily count to _____ .

❖ _____ puede contar con facilidad hasta _____ .

Math

Proficient (Competente) *(cont.)*

◆ _____ is able to demonstrate addition of whole numbers up to 100 with and without regrouping.

❖ _____ es capaz de demostrar la suma de números enteros hasta 100 con y sin reagrupaciones.

◆ _____ understands and computes story problems with great ease.

❖ _____ entiende y resuelve con gran facilidad los problemas planteados en forma de historia.

◆ _____ can easily tell time. He/she helps other students willingly with this task.

❖ _____ puede decir la hora con facilidad. Se muestra dispuesto(a) a ayudar a sus compañeros con esta tarea.

◆ _____ can identify all coins and make change with ease.

❖ _____ puede identificar todas las monedas y hacer cambio con facilidad.

◆ _____ understands and applies knowledge of linear measurement. With this knowledge, he/she can accurately apply measurement strategies to successfully solve problems.

❖ _____ entiende y aplica sus conocimientos de medición lineal. Con estos conocimientos, puede aplicar estrategias de medición de manera correcta para resolver problemas.

◆ _____ understands place value and can easily regroup multi-digit numbers.

❖ _____ entiende los valores posicionales y puede reagrupar con facilidad números de varios dígitos.

◆ _____ is successful in comparing and representing numbers using _____ (fractions, decimals, etc.).

❖ _____ sabe comparar y representar números usando _____ (fracciones, decimales, etc.).

◆ _____ understands and can explain operations in _____.

❖ _____ entiende y puede explicar operaciones en _____ .

◆ _____ can use data analysis and probability to solve problems.

❖ _____ puede usar análisis de datos y probabilidad para resolver problemas.

◆ _____ is successful in comparing, ordering, and representing numbers using _____ (fractions, decimals, factors, or square roots).

❖ _____ sabe comparar, ordenar y representar números usando _____ (fracciones, decimales, factores o raíces cuadradas).

Math

Proficient (Competente) *(cont.)*

◆ _____ recognizes the relationship among radius, diameter, circumference, and area of a circle. He/she can use related formulas in a problem solving context.

❖ _____ reconoce la relación entre radio, diámetro, circunferencia y área de un círculo. Puede usar fórmulas relacionadas para resolver problemas.

Making Progress (Está Progresando)

◆ _____ is steadily improving in math. He/she pays attention in class and completes his/her work with few errors. I am pleased with his/her progress.

❖ _____ mejora continuamente en matemáticas. Pone atención en clase y hace sus tareas con pocos errores. Estoy muy contento(a) con la manera en que ha progresado.

◆ _____ has shown increased interest in math. This is reflected in his/her math scores.

❖ _____ ha demostrado mayor interés por las matemáticas. Esto se refleja en sus calificaciones de esa asignatura.

◆ _____ is beginning to interpret graphs, apply that information, and use it in problem solving.

❖ _____ comienza a interpretar gráficas, a aplicar esa información y a usarla para resolver problemas.

◆ _____ is gaining confidence when he/she works with graphs. Although he/she needs some assistance, he/she can interpret most graphs with accuracy.

❖ _____ demuestra cada vez más seguridad cuando trabaja con gráficas. Aunque necesita un poco de ayuda, puede interpretar con precisión la mayoría de las gráficas.

◆ _____ has memorized all of his/her _____ facts. This impacts his/her ability to complete assignments accurately. Please keep using the flashcards at home each evening to increase speed.

❖ _____ ha memorizado todos los datos de _____ . Esto se refleja en su capacidad de hacer con precisión sus tareas. Por favor sigan usando las tarjetas didácticas en casa todas las tardes para mejorar la velocidad.

◆ _____ understands and uses basic math facts up to _____ . Please use the enclosed flashcards to work on the next the level of facts.

❖ _____ entiende y usa operaciones matemáticas básicas hasta _____ . Por favor usen en su casa las tarjetas didácticas adjuntas para trabajar en el nivel siguiente de operaciones.

◆ _____ is improving in math, but needs to continue to practice _____ facts.

❖ _____ está mejorando en matemáticas, pero necesita seguir practicando las operaciones de _____ .

Math

Making Progress (Está Progresando) *(cont.)*

- ◆ Although _____ is doing well in math, he/she is relying too heavily on a (calculator, math chart, etc.) when computing math facts. Please help him/her practice math facts to mastery.
- ❖ Aunque a _____ le va bien en matemáticas, depende demasiado de (calculadoras, tablas, etc.) cuando hace cálculos. Por favor ayudenlo(a) en su casa a practicar con operaciones matemáticas hasta que las domine.

- ◆ _____'s work is improving. However, he/she still reverses some numbers.
- ❖ Las tareas de _____ están mejorando. Sin embargo, aún invierte algunos números.

- ◆ _____ can write numbers to 100. Remind him/her to correct reversals when you notice them.
- ❖ _____ puede escribir los números hasta el 100. Recuerdenle que corrija los números que invierta cuando los note.

- ◆ _____ now knows _____ of the shapes. Continue to practice at home to master this skill.
- ❖ _____ ahora conoce _____ de las figuras. Debe seguir practicando en su casa para dominar esta destreza.

- ◆ _____ can demonstrate addition and subtraction using manipulatives. With practice, he/she will be able to complete problems without concrete support.
- ❖ _____ puede demostrar sumas y restas usando objetos didácticos. Con práctica, podrá resolver los problemas sin la ayuda de objetos.

- ◆ _____ has a better understanding of word problems. He/she participates more in group discussions and is showing more independence in completing assigned story problems.
- ❖ _____ mejoró su comprensión de problemas expresados en palabras. Participa más en las discusiónes grupales y demuestra más independencia para resolver problemas planteados en forma de historia.

- ◆ Although _____ has made improvement in telling time, he/she needs continued practice.
- ❖ Aunque _____ puede decir la hora con más facilidad, necesita seguir practicando.

- ◆ _____ is more confident now when manipulating coins. Continue to practice making change at home with him/her.
- ❖ _____ muestra más seguridad en el uso de monedas. Es conveniente practicar en su casa con él/ella haciendo cambio con dinero.

Math

Making Progress (Está Progresando) *(cont.)*

◆ With more time and practice, _____ will independently use measurement to solve problems.

❖ Con más tiempo y más práctica, _____ usará la medición para resolver problemas en forma independiente.

◆ With support, _____ can use manipulatives to represent place value. Further practice will help build independence.

❖ Con ayuda, _____ puede usar objetos didácticos para representar valores posicionales. Si practica más, se le ayudará a lograr independencia.

◆ _____ is more successful at problem solving using a variety of data and probability information.

❖ _____ progresó en la resolución de problemas usando diferentes datos e información de probabilidad.

◆ _____ is now showing more proficiency in using calculators.

❖ _____ ahora demuestra más dominio para usar calculadoras.

◆ _____ is now able to explain formulas orally using mathematical vocabulary.

❖ _____ ahora puede explicar fórmulas oralmente usando vocabulario matemático.

Needs Improvement (Necesita Mejorar)

◆ _____ is struggling in math. He/she does not seem to enjoy it at all. We need to continue working on basic skills to build a stronger foundation in math.

❖ _____ está teniendo dificultades en matemáticas. Aparentemente, no le gusta esta asignatura. Es necesario que sigamos trabajando en las destrezas básicas para lograr una base más sólida en matemáticas.

◆ _____ is not attentive during math. Perhaps the material is too difficult, and he/she would benefit from additional help at home and at school.

❖ _____ no presta atención durante la matemática. Tal vez el material sea demasiado difícil y él/ella se beneficiaría con ayuda adicional en su casa y en la escuela.

◆ Encourage _____ to use flashcards and complete all math homework to strengthen skills and develop confidence.

❖ Se debe motivar a _____ para que use las tarjetas didácticas y haga todas las tareas de matemáticas en la casa. Así reforzará sus destrezas y se sentirá más seguro(a).

Math

Needs Improvement (Necesita Mejorar) *(cont.)*

◆ _____ does not understand the concepts in math. Please call me for an appointment to discuss a plan of action.

❖ _____ no entiende los conceptos de matemáticas. Les ruego se comuniquen conmigo para hacer una cita y hablar de las próximas medidas que debemos tomar.

◆ _____ lacks a degree of confidence in math. Extra support and practice at home and at school will build skills and confidence.

❖ _____ necesita sentirse más seguro(a) en matemáticas. Con práctica y ayuda extra en su casa y en la escuela, reforzará sus destrezas y su confianza.

◆ _____ is still struggling with _____ . He/she is relying too heavily on manipulatives and should work on memorizing his/her facts.

❖ _____ sigue teniendo dificultades con _____ . Depende demasiado en objetos didácticos y debería practicar la memorización de los datos.

◆ _____ is having difficulty in math. He/she needs to learn the basic facts. Please use the flashcards nightly.

❖ _____ tiene dificultades en matemáticas. Necesita aprender las operaciones básicas. Por favor usen las tarjetas didácticas en su casa todas las noches.

◆ _____ has/has not memorized all of his/her _____ facts. This impacts _____'s ability to complete assignments accurately.

❖ _____ memorizó/no memorizó todas sus datos de _____ . Esto se refleja en la capacidad de _____ para hacer sus tareas correctamente.

◆ I am sorry to report that _____ does not understand the process of _____ . He/she needs additional help. Please call for an appointment.

❖ Lamento informarles que _____ no entiende el proceso de _____ . Necesita ayuda adicional. Les ruego se comuniquen conmigo para hacer una cita.

◆ _____'s progress in math is not consistent. Although he/she has made some progress, he/she needs to continue reviewing _____ every evening.

❖ Los avances mostrados por _____ no son uniformes. Aunque ha avanzado, necesita seguir repasando _____todas las tardes.

Math

Needs Improvement (Necesita Mejorar) *(cont.)*

◆ _____ needs considerable adult assistance to complete word problems. He/she cannot explain nor complete his/her work without help. Please continue to provide help and support at home until he/she can work more independently.

❖ _____ necesita considerable ayuda de adultos para resolver problemas expresados en palabras. No puede explicar ni hacer sus tareas sin ayuda. Continúen dándole ayuda y apoyo en casa hasta que pueda trabajar sin ayuda.

◆ _____ is struggling with telling time. I have sent home a practice clock. Please work with it nightly.

❖ _____ tiene dificultades para decir la hora. Le he enviado a su casa un reloj de práctica. Es conveniente que practique con el reloj todas las noches.

◆ _____ cannot identify coins. Please practice identifying coins with him/her.

❖ _____ no puede identificar las monedas. Por favor ayudenlo(a) practicar la identificación de monedas.

◆ _____ is unable to successfully demonstrate his/her knowledge when measuring. More practice is needed.

❖ _____ no puede demostrar sus conocimientos al hacer mediciones. Necesita practicar más.

◆ _____ does not understand place value. Until this is mastered, he/she will have difficulty with the more challenging math problems to come. Please help him/her complete the enclosed place value homework packet.

❖ _____ no entiende los valores posicionales. Mientras no los entienda, tendrá dificultades con los problemas matemáticos más complejos que estudiará más adelante. Por favor ayuden(lo/la) hacer las tareas del paquete adjunto de tareas de valores posicionales.

◆ _____ is beginning to make progress in _____ . More time and effort is needed, however, to help him/her reach grade level.

❖ _____ comienza a mostrar avances en _____ . Sin embargo, necesita dedicar más tiempo y esfuerzo para alcanzar el nivel de este grado.

◆ _____ is struggling to make the link between concrete, representational, and abstract.

❖ _____ tiene dificultades para relacionar lo concreto, lo figurativo y lo abstracto.

Oral Language

Proficient (Competente)

◆ _____ uses complex sentences and expresses his/her ideas clearly.

❖ _____ usa oraciones complejas y expresa claramente sus ideas.

◆ _____ has a very high vocabulary, scoring at a _____ grade level. This is apparent in his/her reading, writing, and speaking.

❖ _____ tiene un vocabulario muy elevado, con puntuación de _____ grado. Esto es evidente en la lectura, la escritura y la expresión oral.

◆ _____ is a delightful conversationalist; he/she always contributes to our class discussions.

❖ _____ es un(a) conversador(a) muy agradable. Siempre contribuye a las discusiónes en la clase.

Making Progress (Está Progresando)

◆ _____ speaks with confidence in small groups. With support and practice, this should transfer to a whole-group setting.

❖ _____ muestra seguridad para hablar en pequeños grupos. Con apoyo y práctica, esto puede transferirse al ámbito de todo el grupo.

◆ _____ expresses ideas well during conversations, but this is not transferring to our more formal classroom setting. I plan to provide more small and large group opportunities for discussion.

❖ _____ expresa ideas con claridad en una conversación, pero esto no se transfiere al ámbito más formal del salón de clases. Planeo darle más oportunidades para hablar en grupos pequeños y grandes.

◆ When _____ answers questions at school, he/she is showing improvement in the use of complete sentences. Please continue to reinforce the use of complete sentences at home.

❖ Cuando _____ contesta preguntas en la escuela, demuestra que está mejorando en el uso de oraciones completas. Por favor refuercen este uso en su casa.

Oral Language

Needs Improvement (Necesita Mejorar)

◆ _____ has a very limited vocabulary. Please provide opportunities for conversation at home.

❖ _____ tiene un vocabulario muy limitado. Por favor creenle oportunidades para conversar en su casa.

◆ It is difficult to understand _____ . He/she needs to slow down and speak more clearly to be understood.

❖ Es difícil entenderle a _____ . Necesita hablar con mayor lentitud y claridad.

◆ _____ is having difficulty when speaking in front of others. We need to find opportunities to encourage practice.

❖ A _____ se le dificulta hablar delante de otros. Es necesario que encontremos oportunidades para motivar la práctica.

Reading

Proficient (Competente)

◆ _____ is making excellent progress in reading. He/she is reading well above grade level.

❖ _____ está mostrando un avance excelente en lectura. Tiene un nivel de lectura muy superior al nivel de su grado.

◆ _____ enjoys reading fiction and nonfiction books. This should benefit him/her in all of the academic areas.

❖ A _____ le gusta leer libros de ficción y de no ficción. Esto lo beneficiará en todas las áreas académicas.

◆ _____'s love of reading makes him/her a joy to teach.

❖ El gran entusiasmo por la lectura de _____ hace que enseñarle sea un placer.

◆ _____ is interested in books and reading. He/she often reads for pleasure in class.

❖ A _____ le interesan los libros y la lectura. A menudo lee por placer en clase.

◆ _____ comprehends and follows written directions. He/she is an excellent independent reader.

❖ _____ comprende y sigue las instrucciones escritas. Lee excelentemente sin ayuda.

◆ _____ learns new vocabulary quickly. This allows him/her to choose and understand more challenging books.

❖ _____ aprende vocabulario nuevo rápidamente. Esto le permite elegir y entender libros más difíciles.

◆ Because _____ is a great reader, he/she is doing well in all areas.

❖ Debido a que _____ lee tan bien, está obteniendo buenos resultados en todas las áreas.

◆ _____ asks pertinent questions and participates in story discussions. He/she is a leader in our classroom.

❖ _____ hace preguntas adecuadas y participa en las discusiónes sobre relatos. Es líder en nuestro salón de clases.

◆ _____ knows all the letters and sounds of the alphabet. He/she is now beginning to decode words.

❖ _____ conoce todas las letras y sonidos del alfabeto. Ahora está empezando a leer palabras.

◆ _____ blends short words without assistance. He/she is ready for more challenging words.

❖ _____ combina palabras cortas sin ayuda. Está listo(a) para palabras más difíciles.

Reading

Proficient (Competente) *(cont.)*

◆ _____ can produce rhymes and identify beginning and ending sounds. He/she is working above grade level in these areas.

❖ _____ puede crear rimas e identificar los sonidos iniciales y finales. Está trabajando por encima del nivel del grado en estas áreas.

◆ _____ is an independent reader. He/she has a great love for reading that will benefit him/her throughout his/her life.

❖ _____ lee en forma independiente. Le gusta mucho leer y eso será un beneficio para toda su vida.

◆ _____ is an excellent reader. He/she uses a variety of strategies and self corrects errors.

❖ _____ lee excelentemente. Usa diversas estrategias y se corrige a sí mismo(a).

◆ _____ is a dynamic, eager reader. His/her insightful comments during class discussions help everyone gain a better understanding of the story.

❖ _____ es un(a) lector(a) muy activo(a) y entusiasta. Sus inteligentes comentarios durante las discusiónes de clase ayudan a que todos entiendan mejor los relatos.

◆ _____ has done well this semester. He/she shows great enthusiasm for reading.

❖ A _____ le ha ido bien este semestre. Muestra gran entusiasmo por la lectura.

◆ _____ catches on quickly to new reading skills. This is helping him/her become a proficient reader.

❖ _____ entiende rápidamente las nuevas destrezas de lectura. Esto le ayudará a que sea muy competente para leer.

◆ _____ excels in reading. He/she is willing to take risks and choose challenging books to read.

❖ _____ se destaca en lectura. No teme asumir riesgos ni elegir libros difíciles para leer.

◆ I am pleased with the progress that _____ has made in reading. His/her strong skills and solid foundation have made him/her a great reader.

❖ Me alegra ver el progreso que _____ tuvo en lectura. Sus fuertes destrezas y bases sólidas le permiten leer muy bien.

◆ It is a delight to listen to _____ read. He/she reads clearly and with expression.

❖ Es un placer escuchar cómo lee _____. Lo hace con claridad y expresión.

Reading

Proficient (Competente) *(cont.)*

◆ _____ enjoys reading poetry and short stories aloud in groups. This is helping other students discover the joy of reading.

❖ A _____ le gusta leer poesía y relatos cortos en voz alta en grupo. Esto ayuda a que otros estudiantes descubran el placer de la lectura.

◆ I enjoy reading _____'s summaries. They are very detailed.

❖ Es un placer leer los resúmenes de _____ . Son muy detallados.

◆ _____ effectively communicates the main idea of a story and summarizes with rich, vivid detail.

❖ _____ expresa muy bien la idea principal de un relato y hace resúmenes detallados y descriptivos.

◆ _____ is able to respond to literature in number of ways. I enjoy his/her projects.

❖ _____ puede responder a la literatura de diferentes formas. Es un placer leer sus trabajos.

Making Progress (Está Progresando)

◆ _____'s comprehension has greatly improved. To help at home, have him/her retell stories as he/she reads them.

❖ _____ ha mejorado mucho su nivel de comprensión. Para ayudarlo(a) en casa, se le debe pedir que cuente con sus propias palabras los relatos que lee.

◆ _____ is reading fluently but does not comprehend what he/she reads. When _____ reads at home, ask him/her questions about the story.

❖ _____ lee con fluidez, pero no comprende lo que lee. Cuando _____ lea en su casa, haganle preguntas sobre el relato.

◆ _____ is improving in reading. Thank you for your support.

❖ _____ está mejorando en lectura. Muchas gracias por su apoyo.

◆ _____'s reading is showing improvement. Have him/her read to younger children for additional practice. This should result in further gains.

❖ _____ está mejorando en lectura. Pídanle que lea para niños más pequeños, a fin de que practique más. Esto será muy beneficioso.

◆ _____'s reading is beginning to improve. Continue to expose him/her to a wide variety of materials.

❖ _____ comienza a mejorar en lectura. Se le debe seguir dando diverso material para que practique en su casa.

Reading

Making Progress (Está Progresando) *(cont.)*

◆ _____'s reading is slow, but he/she comprehends the text. To increase his/her speed, have him/her orally read the same passage multiple times.

❖ _____ lee lentamente, pero comprende el texto. Para que aumente la velocidad, hagan que lea el mismo pasaje varias veces en voz alta en su casa.

◆ _____ is learning to attack words independently. He/she is now using more decoding skills.

❖ _____ está aprendiendo a leer palabras por separado. Ahora está usando más destrezas de lectura.

◆ _____ can now recognize _____ sight words. Continue using the flashcards for more progress.

❖ _____ ahora puede reconocer _____ palabras a primera vista. Por favor sigan usando tarjetas didácticas en su casa para que progrese más.

◆ Thank you for talking to _____ about paying attention in class. He/she focuses more on his/her work. As a result, his/her reading has improved.

❖ Muchas gracias por hablar con _____ para que ponga atención en clase. Ahora se concentra más en sus tareas. En consecuencia, ha mejorado en lectura.

◆ _____'s reading is becoming more fluent. Keep reading at home. Your help is appreciated!

❖ _____ lee con más fluidez. Debe seguir leyendo en su casa. ¡Muchas gracias por la ayuda!

◆ _____ is beginning to read words in phrases; this is helping his/her fluency.

❖ _____ comienza a leer palabras dentro de frases. Esto mejora su fluidez.

◆ _____ does well on reading tests, but he/she does not seem to enjoy reading. We need to help him/her develop a love for reading by guiding him/her to books that reflect his/her interests.

❖ A _____ le va bien en exámenes de lectura, pero parece que no le gusta leer. Es necesario que lo(a) orientemos para que encuentre libros de su interés y descubra el placer de leer.

◆ _____ knows all the letters of the alphabet, but I am still concerned about his/her phonemic awareness skills. Please practice rhyming and beginning sounds at home.

❖ _____ conoce todas las letras del alfabeto, pero me preocupan sus destrezas para diferenciar sonidos. Debe practicar con rimas y sonidos iniciales en su casa.

Reading

Making Progress (Está Progresando) *(cont.)*

◆ _____ recognizes most of the uppercase letters, but just a few lowercase letters. Help him/her match uppercase and lowercase letters during flashcard practice to reinforce lowercase recognition.

❖ _____ reconoce la mayoría de las mayúsculas, pero sólo algunas minúsculas. Debe practicar con tarjetas didácticas en su casa para que asocie las mayúsculas con las minúsculas.

◆ _____ is an emergent reader. He/she is showing great effort. Continue reading with him/her at home.

❖ _____ está aprendiendo a leer. Muestra un gran esfuerzo. Ustedes deben seguir leyendo con él/ella en su casa.

◆ _____ has improved steadily in reading. He/she is capable of utilizing more reading strategies now.

❖ _____ ha mejorado constantemente en lectura. Ahora puede usar más estrategias para leer.

◆ _____ can identify sight words in isolation but cannot easily recognize them when reading. More practice is needed.

❖ _____ puede identificar palabras aisladas a primera vista, pero no puede reconocerlas fácilmente cuando lee. Necesita practicar más.

◆ _____ now knows and can use the letter sounds. Thank you for your help.

❖ _____ ahora conoce los sonidos de las letras y los puede usar. Muchas gracias por su ayuda.

◆ _____ is gaining independence in reading, however, he/she needs to work towards fluency.

❖ _____ lee en forma más independiente. Sin embargo, necesita practicar para leer con más fluidez.

◆ _____ can decode simple stories but is not reading with expression. He/she needs to practice reading aloud frequently.

❖ _____ puede leer relatos simples, pero necesita darles expresión. Necesita practicar con frecuencia la lectura en voz alta.

◆ _____ has blossomed this year and is becoming an independent reader. He/she has become more confident in his/her reading abilities.

❖ _____ ha mejorado este año y está aprendiendo a leer en forma independiente. Muestra más seguridad en sus capacidades de lectura.

Reading

Making Progress (Está Progresando) *(cont.)*

- ◆ _____ is currently reading at grade level, but strengthening his/her comprehension skills will help him/her excel in reading.

- ❖ _____ actualmente tiene el nivel de lectura de este grado, pero si refuerza sus destrezas de comprensión, se destacará en lectura.

- ◆ _____ does not understand the importance of phonic skills and depends heavily on sight reading. We need to address this problem so _____ can realize his/her great academic potential.

- ❖ _____ no entiende la importancia de las destrezas para pronunciar los sonidos y depende mucho de la lectura visual. Es necesario que nos ocupemos de este problema para que _____ pueda desarrollar sus grandes aptitudes académicas.

- ◆ I am pleased that _____ has made progress in reading. He/she will soon be on grade level. Thank you for your help.

- ❖ Me alegra ver que _____ ha progresado en lectura. Pronto estará en el nivel de este grado. Muchas gracias por su ayuda.

- ◆ _____'s progress has been amazing! His/her reading scores have increased more than anyone's in the class.

- ❖ ¡Los avances de _____ han sido asombrosos! Sus calificaciones en lectura son las que más mejoraron en la clase.

- ◆ _____'s summarizing skills have improved and as a result, his/her comprehension has improved.

- ❖ Las destrezas para resumir de _____ han mejorado. Como resultado, también mejoró su comprensión.

- ◆ Through practice, _____ is now able to summarize more effectively.

- ❖ Gracias a la práctica, _____ ahora puede hacer mejores resúmenes.

- ◆ _____'s ability to analyze a passage has improved. We will continue to work on this skill in class.

- ❖ La capacidad de _____ para analizar un pasaje ha mejorado. Seguiremos trabajando en esa destreza en clase.

- ◆ _____ is now able to identify the main ideas in a story in his/her summaries.

- ❖ _____ ahora puede identificar las ideas principales de un relato e incluirlas en un resumen.

Reading

Making Progress (Está Progresando) *(cont.)*

◆ _____ is now able to offer direct responses to his/her reading with reasons, examples, and details.

❖ _____ ahora puede responder directamente a sus lecturas y dar razones, ejemplos y detalles.

◆ _____ now participates in literature circles with more confidence.

❖ _____ ahora participa en círculos de literatura con más seguridad.

◆ _____'s presentations are more interesting now that he/she uses an outline to organize his/her thoughts.

❖ Las presentaciones de _____ son más interesantes ahora porque usa un esquema para organizar sus ideas.

◆ _____ is able to analyze the elements of a story and can now draw conclusions.

❖ _____ puede analizar los elementos de un relato y sacar conclusiones.

◆ _____ is now able to discuss the text, summarize the key points, and make an outline.

❖ _____ ahora puede hablar del texto, resumir los puntos importantes y hacer un esquema.

Needs Improvement (Necesita Mejorar)

◆ _____ is having difficulty in reading. He/she needs to increase in his/her fluency. Please have him/her read aloud to you each evening.

❖ _____ tiene dificultades para leer. Necesita mejorar su fluidez. Debe leerles a ustedes en voz alta todas las tardes.

◆ _____ is struggling with reading. For him/her to improve, he/she needs to read more at home.

❖ _____ tiene dificultades con la lectura. Para mejorar, necesita leer más en su casa.

◆ Although _____ hesitates to read in a group, his/her oral reading is good. Have him/her read aloud at home to build confidence.

❖ Aunque _____ duda cuando lee en un grupo, su lectura oral es buena. Debe leer en voz alta en su casa para que sienta más seguridad.

◆ _____ has a great deal of trouble paying attention during reading. I am worried that he/she is missing critical elements. We need to schedule a conference to develop a plan for him/her.

❖ _____ tiene dificultades para poner atención cuando lee. Me preocupa que pueda perderse elementos muy importantes. Es necesario que programemos una cita para hablar de lo que podemos hacer.

Reading

Needs Improvement (Necesita Mejorar) *(cont.)*

◆ _____ needs assistance with most reading skills. He/she needs more time devoted to practicing reading skills.

❖ _____ necesita ayuda con la mayoría de sus destrezas de lectura. Necesita dedicar más tiempo a la práctica de estas destrezas.

◆ _____ does not comprehend simple stories. I will be calling for a conference.

❖ _____ no comprende los relatos sencillos. Me comunicaré con ustedes para que tengamos una reunión.

◆ _____ does not willingly participate in reading activities. We need to help him/her develop more skills so reading is easier. We should also help him/her choose interesting books so reading is more enjoyable.

❖ _____ no muestra disposición para participar en actividades de lectura. Es necesario que lo(a) ayudemos a desarrollar más estrategias para que leer le resulte más fácil. También es necesario que lo(a) ayudemos a elegir libros interesantes para que disfrute de la lectura.

◆ _____ misinterprets context clues and needs assistance making connections between idea and details. This is affecting his/her comprehension. Have him/her re-tell fairy tales and other familiar stories with as many details as possible to develop this skill.

❖ _____ no interpreta bien las pistas del contexto y necesita ayuda para relacionar una idea y los detalles. Esto afecta su comprensión. Para desarrollar esta destreza, es conveniente que en su casa narre con sus propias palabras los relatos o cuentos que lee, con todos los detalles posibles.

◆ _____ is not retaining _____ . He/she needs more repetition and practice at home.

❖ _____ no retiene _____ . Él/ella necesita más repetición y practica en su casa.

◆ _____ cannot blend sounds into words. He/she may have an auditory problem. We should have him/her tested.

❖ _____ no puede combinar sonidos para formar palabras. Tal vez tenga algún problema auditivo y sea conveniente que le realicemos pruebas audivitivas.

◆ _____ is having difficulty with basic phonics skills. I will send home a packet of work that should improve these skills. Please complete it with him/her.

❖ _____ tiene dificultades con las destrezas para pronunciar los sonidos básicos. Le enviaré a su casa un paquete de prácticas que pueden mejorar esas destrezas. Por favor completen el paquete con él/ella.

Reading

Needs Improvement (Necesita Mejorar) *(cont.)*

◆ _____ does not enjoy reading. He/she needs frequent encouragement. Please read with him/her at home to build a love for reading.

❖ A _____ no le gusta leer. Necesita motivación frecuente. Por favor lean con él/ella en su casa para que descubra el placer de la lectura.

◆ _____ is having difficulty expressing the main idea of a story. I am concerned with his/her level of comprehension.   Have him/her identify the main idea of fairy tales or favorite stories to strengthen this skill.

❖ _____ tiene dificultades para expresar la idea principal de un relato. Me preocupa su nivel de comprensión. Para reforzar esta destreza, es conveniente que en su casa identifique la idea principal de sus relatos o cuentos favoritos.

◆ _____ does not recognize the letters of the alphabet. He/she is working below grade level. Please use the flashcards that I am sending home to practice letter recognition nightly.

❖ _____ no reconoce todas las letras del alfabeto. Está trabajando por debajo del nivel de este grado. Por favor usen las tarjetas didácticas que estoy enviando a su casa para que practique el reconocimiento de las letras todas las noches.

◆ _____ does not recognize rhymes and is struggling to identify initial consonant sounds. Perhaps this is related to his/her speech problems. Continue to provide support at home.

❖ _____ no reconoce las rimas y tiene dificultades para identificar los sonidos de las consonantes iniciales. Tal vez esto tenga relación con sus dificultades para hablar. Es conveniente que se le siga dando apoyo en su casa.

◆ _____ is weak in basic reading skills. He/she needs to practice alphabet recognition, rhyming, and beginning sounds daily.

❖ _____ tiene dificultades con las destrezas básicas de lectura. Necesita practicar diariamente con rimas, sonidos iniciales y el reconocimiento del alfabeto.

◆ _____ demonstrates letter-sound knowledge. However, he/she cannot yet transfer that knowledge when decoding words. We will continue to practice decoding in small groups.

❖ _____ demuestra que conoce los sonidos de las letras. Sin embargo, todavía no puede transferir ese conocimiento para leer palabras. Seguiremos practicando lectura en grupos pequeños.

◆ With a better attitude toward reading, _____ would enjoy reading more.

❖ Si _____ mejorara su actitud hacia la lectura, le gustaría más leer.

Reading

Needs Improvement (Necesita Mejorar) *(cont.)*

◆ _____ needs to work on vocabulary words more at home. This will help him/her become a better reader.

❖ _____ necesita trabajar más con vocabulario en su casa. Esto ayudará a que pueda leer mejor.

◆ _____ does not recognize many sight words. He/she needs to use the flashcards at home.

❖ _____ no reconoce muchas palabras cuando lee a primera vista. Necesita usar las tarjetas didácticas en su casa.

◆ _____ is having difficulty with letter sounds. He frequently confuses the sounds of _____ and _____ . Please review sounds at home.

❖ _____ tiene dificultades con los sonidos de las letras. Con frecuencia, confunde los sonidos de _____ y _____ . Debe repasar los sonidos en su casa.

◆ Please continue working with _____ at home, reading at least 20 minutes a night. Please focus on comprehension strategies. Thank you for your support!

❖ Por favor sigan trabajando con _____ en su casa, leyendo al menos 20 minutos por la noche y haciendo hincapié en estrategias de comprensión. ¡Muchas gracias por su apoyo!

◆ _____ does not enjoy reading aloud. I won't call on him/her to read in front of a group, but he/she needs to read aloud to you and me to build fluency.

❖ A _____ no le gusta leer en voz alta. No lo(a) llamaré a leer frente al grupo, pero necesita leer en voz alta para ustedes y para mí a fin de que logre fluidez.

◆ _____ is struggling with summarizing. Please have him/her practice retelling stories at home.

❖ _____ tiene dificultades para resumir. Es conveniente que practique en su casa narrando con sus propias palabras los relatos que lee.

◆ _____ has difficulty analyzing his/her reading. We will focus on this during the next grading period.

❖ _____ tiene dificultades para analizar sus lecturas. Nos concentraremos en esto durante el siguiente período de evaluación.

◆ _____ makes unsupported responses in the literature circle.

❖ _____ da respuestas sin fundamentos en el círculo de literatura.

◆ _____ responds inconsistently and inappropriately in our literature discussions.

❖ _____ da respuestas poco adecuadas y con poco fundamento en nuestras discusiónes de literatura.

Science

Proficient (Competente)

◆ _____ shows an understanding of all of the scientific concepts we have studied this period.

❖ _____ demuestra que entiende todos los conceptos científicos que estudiamos en este período.

◆ _____ is highly engaged in science. He/she uses science materials and equipment correctly to solve problems.

❖ _____ muestra gran dedicación en ciencias. Usa el material y el equipo de la asignatura correctamente para resolver problemas.

◆ _____ displays an enthusiasm for science. He/she can predict an outcome and test his/her hypothesis through experimentation. He/she can draw conclusions based on his/her observations.

❖ _____ demuestra entusiasmo por las ciencias. Puede predecir un resultado y poner a prueba sus hipótesis a través de la experimentación. Puede sacar conclusiones basadas en sus observaciones.

Making Progress (Está Progresando)

◆ _____ is showing a better understanding of science. He/she participates more in the science activities.

❖ _____ demuestra que entiende mejor las ciencias y participa más en las actividades.

◆ _____ is applying more skills and strategies and seems to be more aware of safety procedures.

❖ _____ aplica más destrezas y estrategias y parece comprender mejor los procedimientos de seguridad.

◆ I am pleased with _____'s progress in science. He/she is making better observations and beginning to record data and show a deeper understanding of the scientific processes.

❖ Me alegra ver los avances de _____ en ciencias. Ha mejorado sus observaciones. También comienza a registrar datos y a demostrar una comprensión más profunda de los procesos científicos.

Science

Needs Improvement (Necesita Mejorar)

◆ _____ does not understand basic science concepts. We need to encourage him/her to take more interest in science.

❖ _____ no entiende los conceptos científicos básicos. Es necesario que lo(a) motivemos para que se interese más en esta asignatura.

◆ _____ needs to pay attention more during our science activities. He/she is easily distracted, and therefore cannot draw conclusions based on observations.

❖ _____ necesita poner más atención en nuestras actividades de ciencias. Se distrae fácilmente y por esa razón no puede sacar conclusiones basadas en sus observaciones.

◆ _____ needs to be encouraged to take risks in scientific endeavors. He/she has difficulty making predictions or drawing conclusions.

❖ _____ necesita motivación para que se atreva a asumir riesgos en sus actividades de ciencias. Tiene dificultades para hacer predicciones y sacar conclusiones.

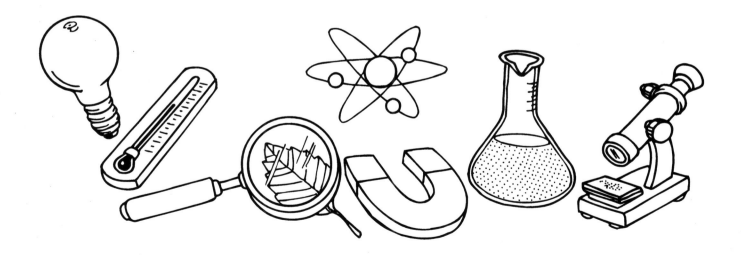

Social Studies

Proficient (Competente)

◆ _____ communicates the knowledge he/she has gained in social studies. His/her last project was exceptional.

❖ _____ comunica el conocimiento que adquiere en estudios sociales. Su último trabajo fue excepcional.

◆ _____'s reference skills are superior.

❖ Las destrezas de _____ para usar material de referencia son sobresalientes.

◆ _____ is very interested in current events. This is contributing to him/her becoming a well-rounded citizen.

❖ _____ muestra gran interés en los acontecimientos de actualidad. Esto contribuye a su formación como un(a) ciudadano(a) bien informado(a).

Making Progress (Está Progresando)

◆ _____ has greatly improved in social studies. However, he/she needs to participate more in classroom discussions.

❖ _____ ha mejorado mucho en estudios sociales. Sin embargo, debe participar más en las discusiónes de clase.

◆ _____ is showing a greater interest in social studies. However, he/she did not turn in his/her last project, and this affected his/her grade.

❖ _____ muestra mayor interés en estudios sociales. Sin embargo no entregó su último proyecto y esto afectó sus calificaciones.

◆ It is great to see that _____ is showing more effort in social studies. His/her last (map, project, paper, etc.) was delightful.

❖ Es fantástico ver que _____ demuestra más esfuerzo en estudios sociales. Su último (mapa, trabajo, etc.) fue estupendo.

Social Studies

Needs Improvement (Necesita Mejorar)

◆ _____ has difficulty interpreting maps. Help _____ make simple maps of your home and other familiar places to develop this skill.

❖ _____ tiene dificultades para interpretar mapas. Para desarrollar esta destreza, es necesario ayudar a _____ a que dibuje mapas simples de su casa y de otros lugares conocidos.

◆ Please encourage _____ to pay better attention during social studies. He/she is off task during our whole-group instruction, and this is affecting his/her ability to complete social studies assignments.

❖ Por favor animen a _____ para que ponga más atención en estudios sociales. Se distrae en las actividades de todo el grupo y esto afecta su capacidad de hacer las tareas de estudios sociales.

◆ _____ is not turning in his/her social studies homework. This is affecting his/her grade. Please encourage him/her to complete it and turn it in.

❖ _____ no está entregando sus tareas de estudios sociales. Esto está afectando sus calificaciones. Por favor motivenlo(a) en casa para que las haga y las entregue.

Spelling

Proficient (Competente)

◆ I am pleased that _____ is serious about spelling. He/she is well prepared for all tests, and this transfers to his/her written work.

❖ Me alegra ver que _____ toma en serio el deletreo de palabras. Está muy bien preparado(a) para todos los exámenes y esto se refleja en sus tareas escritas.

◆ _____ is a great speller! I would like to encourage him/her to try out for the spelling bee. I am sending home a list of words to begin his/her study.

❖ ¡ _____ deletrea muy bien las palabras! Me gustaría motivarlo(a) para que se presente a la competencia de deletreo. Le envío a su casa una lista de palabras para que comience a estudiar.

◆ _____ has achieved excellent scores on our weekly spelling tests.

❖ _____ ha alcanzado excelentes calificaciones en nuestros exámenes semanales de deletreo.

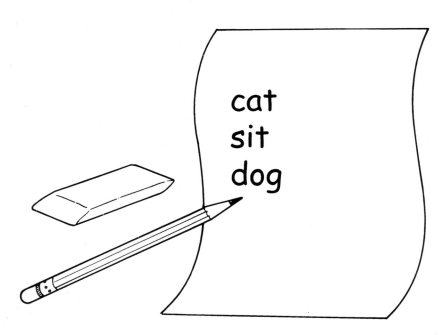

Spelling

Making Progress (Está Progresando)

◆ _____'s spelling has greatly improved, but he/she needs to continue working in this subject. Please help him/her practice spelling words nightly.

❖ La ortografía de _____ ha mejorado mucho, pero necesita seguir trabajando en ella. Por favor ayudenlo(a) a practicar el deletreo de palabras todas las noches.

◆ Please continue to practice spelling words with _____ . This has made a significant difference in his/her test scores.

❖ Por favor sigan practicando el deletreo de palabras con _____ . Esto mejorará significativamente las calificaciones de sus exámenes.

◆ _____ is becoming a great speller. He/she is using an understanding of word families to help him/her spell related words.

❖ _____ comienza a deletrear muy bien. Usa sus conocimientos de familias de palabras para ayudarse a deletrear palabras relacionadas.

Needs Improvement (Necesita Mejorar)

◆ _____ is having a difficult time in spelling. To build success, I would like to give him/her fewer words. Please call me so we can discuss this.

❖ _____ tiene problemas para deletrear. Para ayudarlo(a), me gustaría darle menos palabras. Les ruego se comuniquen conmigo para que hablemos de esto.

◆ _____ needs to focus more on his/her spelling words. He/she frequently makes careless errors.

❖ _____ necesita concentrarse más en deletrear palabras. El/ella frequentemente hace errores negligentes.

◆ _____ is struggling in spelling. He/she does not follow any spelling rules, and he/she is not memorizing his/her words. Please review the enclosed spelling rules with _____ and help him/her memorize the weekly spelling list.

❖ _____ tiene dificultades para deletrear. No sigue las reglas de ortografía y no memoriza las palabras asignadas. Por favor revisen las reglas adjuntas con _____ para ayudarlo(a) a memorizar su lista semanal de deletreo.

Writing

Proficient (Competente)

◆ _____ utilizes a variety of resources as he/she writes organized and creative stories.

❖ _____ usa diferentes recursos para escribir relatos creativos y bien organizados.

◆ _____ demonstrates critical thinking in writing. He/she also expresses his/her ideas clearly and concisely.

❖ _____ demuestra tener pensamiento crítico en sus redacciones. También expresa sus ideas en forma clara y concisa.

◆ _____ excels in writing. He/she drafts ideas fluently, then revises and proofreads to produce a final copy that is accurate, unified, and consistent.

❖ _____ se destaca en redacción. Escribe borradores de ideas con fluidez, luego los revisa y corrige. El resultado final tiene precisión, unidad y coherencia.

◆ _____ can self-edit. He/she is ready to publish after editing.

❖ _____ puede corregir su propio trabajo y muestra disposición para publicarlo.

Making Progress (Está Progresando)

◆ I am pleased that _____'s writing has improved. He/she still needs assistance when revising, but he/she is becoming more independent.

❖ Me alegra ver que la redacción de _____ ha mejorado. Aún necesita ayuda para revisar su trabajo, pero está logrando más independencia.

◆ Although _____ needs some help planning and organizing his/her writing, once he/she begins the actual writing he/she is very creative.

❖ Aunque _____ necesita un poco de ayuda para planear y organizar sus redacciones, cuando comienza a escribir muestra gran creatividad.

◆ _____ is becoming an accomplished writer. Compare the attached writing samples to notice an overall improvement.

❖ _____ comienza a escribir muy bien. Comparen las muestras de redacción adjuntas para apreciar su avance general.

◆ _____'s editing has improved now that he/she is utilizing more resources.

❖ _____ ha mejorado sus correcciones y usa más recursos.

Writing

Needs Improvement (Necesita Mejorar)

◆ _____ does not willingly participate in writing activities. He/she should be encouraged to keep a daily journal or writing log.

❖ _____ no muestra disposición para participar en las actividades de redacción. Es necesario motivarlo(a) para que todos los días escriba en un cuaderno o diario de redacción.

◆ _____ makes many errors in spelling when writing. He/she needs to learn to use resources (spell check, dictionaries, spelling lists, etc.) to correct errors.

❖ _____ comete muchos errores de ortografía. Necesita aprender a usar distintos recursos (verificación ortográfica, diccionarios, listas de ortografía, etc.) para corregir los errores.

◆ _____ has difficulty organizing information. He/she needs to spend more time planning his/her writing.

❖ _____ tiene dificultades para organizar la información. Necesita dedicar más tiempo a la planificación de sus redacciones.

◆ _____ needs a lot of support when editing. He/she cannot find his/her own mistakes.

❖ _____ necesita mucho apoyo para hacer las correcciones. No puede encontrar sus propios errores.

◆ To help _____ improve his/her editing skills, I plan to provide opportunities for him to edit with a peer.

❖ Para ayudar a que _____ mejore sus destrezas de corrección, planeo darle oportunidades para que corrija con un(a) compañero(a).

Additional Areas

Proficient (Competente)

- ◆ _____ enjoys all areas of P.E. He/she displays excellent coordination, agility, and skill.
- ❖ A _____ le gustan todas las áreas de educación física. Demuestra excelente coordinación, agilidad y destreza.

- ◆ _____ responds enthusiastically to all tasks and challenges in P.E. He/she works well with other children and is a well-liked team member.
- ❖ _____ responde con entusiasmo a todas las tareas y desafíos de educación física. Trabaja muy bien con otros niños y es muy popular entre los miembros de su equipo.

- ◆ _____ is a talented artist. His/her work is colorful and interesting. I hope he/she will continue to study and develop his/her natural ability.
- ❖ _____ es un(a) artista talentoso(a). Su trabajo es colorido e interesante. Espero que siga estudiando para desarrollar su capacidad natural.

- ◆ _____ enjoys art and participates with enthusiasm. His/her work exhibits creativity.
- ❖ A _____ le gusta el arte y participa con entusiasmo. Su trabajo demuestra creatividad.

- ◆ _____ loves musical activities. If you are able to provide music lessons, he/she would greatly benefit from them.
- ❖ A _____ le gustan mucho las actividades musicales. Si pudiera tomar lecciones de música, éstas serían un gran beneficio para él/ella.

Making Progress (Está Progresando)

- ◆ _____ is developing confidence in all areas of P.E. He/she can now _____ .
- ❖ _____ está desarrollando seguridad en todas las áreas de educación física. Ahora puede _____ .

- ◆ _____ is learning to express him/herself through art. As a result, he/she enjoys the class more and is less disruptive.
- ❖ _____ está aprendiendo a expresarse a través del arte. En consecuencia, le gustan más las clases y tiene un mejor comportamiento.

- ◆ _____ is beginning to develop confidence and coordination. If he/she practices _____, he/she will continue to improve.
- ❖ _____ comienza a desarrollar seguridad y coordinación. Si practica _____ , seguirá mejorando.

Additional Areas

Needs Improvement (Necesita Mejorar)

- ◆ _____ is a talented musician. However, his/her lack of dedication is affecting his/her musical development.

- ❖ _____ tiene talento para la música. Sin embargo, su falta de dedicación está afectando su desarrollo musical.

- ◆ It is obvious when _____ practices at home. Please encourage him/her to schedule a regular practice time if he/she intends to remain involved in music classes.

- ❖ Es evidente cuando _____ practica en su casa. Por favor motivenlo(a) para que programe tiempos de práctica regular si desea seguir participando en las clases de música.

- ◆ _____ has difficulty with his/her coordination and does not seem to enjoy P.E.

- ❖ _____ tiene dificultades de coordinación y parece que no le gusta la educación física.

- ◆ _____ has a natural ability in sports. However, he/she needs to develop sportsmanship.

- ❖ _____ tiene una habilidad natural para los deportes. Sin embargo, necesita desarrollar el espíritu deportivo.

Personal Development

Although academic performance comments are essential, a report card is more complete if it also includes remarks about the student's personal development. The explanation for academic performance, in fact, is often directly related to a particular behavior or study skill.

In the following section, the comments address the student's personal development. They can be used in conjunction with academic comments as an explanation or as general, stand-alone comments about the student.

The subjects addressed in this section include attendance and tardiness, attitude toward school, behavior inside and outside, effort in class, self-confidence, social skills, and work habits. Once again, most sections are divided into "Proficient," "Making Progress," and "Needs Improvement" to facilitate the location of an appropriate comment.

Attendance

Tardiness

- ◆ When _____ is tardy, he/she disturbs the learning of everyone in the classroom. He/she also loses valuable learning time, which is affecting his/her work. Please help _____ arrive in a timely manner.

- ❖ Cuando _____ llega tarde, perturba el aprendizaje del resto de los alumnos. Además, pierde un valioso tiempo para aprender, lo cual afecta su trabajo. Por favor ayuden a _____ a llegar a tiempo.

- ◆ Frequent late arrivals affect _____'s academic performance. He/she misses important information each time he/she is late. Your support is needed in this area.

- ❖ Las frecuentes llegadas tarde de _____ afectan su rendimiento académico. Cada vez que llega tarde, pierde importante información. Se necesita que ustedes lo(a) ayuden en esta área.

- ◆ _____ has been tardy for school _____ times. Because of this, he/she has missed _____ . He/she needs to be at school by _____ A.M. each day.

- ❖ _____ ha llegado tarde a la escuela _____ veces. Por esa razón, ha perdido _____ . Necesita llegar a la escuela antes de las _____ A.M. todos los días.

- ◆ _____ is often tardy. Arriving on time for the school day is very important for student success.

- ❖ _____ a menudo llega tarde. Llegar a tiempo a la escuela es muy importante para el éxito de los alumnos.

- ◆ _____ is a joy to teach. He/she arrives at school on time and ready to learn.

- ❖ Es un placer enseñarle a _____ . Llega a la escuela a tiempo y con buena disposición para aprender.

Absences

- ◆ _____ learns a lot when present, but frequent absences cause gaps in his/her learning. Please make sure _____ is present each day.

- ❖ _____ aprende mucho cuando viene a clase, pero sus ausencias frecuentes causan interrupciones en su aprendizaje. Por favor asegurense de que _____ venga a clase todos los días.

- ◆ We need to schedule a time when you can bring _____ to school. Because of his/her frequent absences, I have not been able to completely evaluate his/her progress.

- ❖ Es necesario que programemos un horario en el que ustedes puedan traer a _____ a la escuela. Debido a sus ausencias frecuentes, no he podido evaluar completamente sus avances.

Attendance

Absences *(cont.)*

- ◆ _____'s frequent absences make it difficult for him/her to stay on grade level. He/she seems tired and often complains about not feeling well. Perhaps _____ should see a doctor.

- ❖ Las ausencias frecuentes de _____ le dificultan permanecer en el nivel de este grado. Parece estar cansado(a) y a menudo se queja de no sentirse bien. Quizás debería consultar al médico.

- ◆ Even though _____ completes homework assignments when absent, he/she misses important social interactions and academic activities that make learning complete. Please try to increase _____'s attendance rate.

- ❖ Aunque _____ hace sus tareas para la casa cuando falta a clase, pierde importante interacciones sociales y actividades académicas que son necesarias para un aprendizaje integral. Es conveniente tratar de que _____ mejore su asistencia a la escuela.

- ◆ _____ has missed _____ days this semester. Because learning is sequential, these absences are affecting his/her academic performance. His/her grades would improve with better attendance.

- ❖ _____ ha faltado _____ días este semestre. Debido a que el aprendizaje necesita continuidad, estas ausencias afectan su rendimiento académico. Sus calificaciones mejorarían si mejorara su asistencia a la escuela.

- ◆ _____ is often absent from class. He/she shows promise in _____ but needs to attend regularly to reach his/her potential.

- ❖ _____ falta con frecuencia. Demuestra aptitudes para _____ , pero necesita asistir a clases regularmente para desarrollarlas.

- ◆ _____ has been in class and on time every day this grading period. This is reflected in his/her work.

- ❖ _____ ha asistido a clase y ha llegado a tiempo en este período de evaluación. Esto se refleja en sus tareas.

- ◆ _____'s attendance is commended. Thank you for your support.

- ❖ La asistencia a clase de _____ es muy meritoria. Muchas gracias por su apoyo.

- ◆ It is a pleasure to see _____ in class each day. His/her attendance is excellent.

- ❖ Me alegra ver a _____ en clase todos los días. Su asistencia es excelente.

Attitude

Proficient (Competente)

◆ _____ has made a good adjustment to _____ grade. His/her attitude toward school is excellent.

❖ _____ se ha adaptado muy bien al _____ grado. Su actitud hacia la escuela es excelente.

◆ _____ is an enthusiastic participant in all of our activities. He/she exhibits a good attitude toward school.

❖ _____ participa con entusiasmo en todas las actividades. Demuestra una buena actitud hacia la escuela.

◆ With _____'s fine attitude and pleasant personality, he/she is a delight to teach.

❖ Es un placer enseñar a alguien con la excelente actitud y agradable personalidad de _____ .

◆ _____ assumes responsibility well and has a good attitude. He/she is cooperative and happy.

❖ _____ asume adecuadamente sus responsabilidades y tiene una buena actitud. Se muestra alegre y colaborador(a).

Making Progress (Está Progresando)

◆ Although _____ has struggled in _____ , he/she has shown a positive attitude about trying to improve in this area.

❖ Aunque _____ ha tenido dificultades en _____ , ha demostrado una actitud positiva para tratar de mejorar en esta área.

◆ _____ is developing a better attitude. He/she now accepts responsibility and is showing interest and enthusiasm for school.

❖ _____ está desarrollando una mejor actitud. Ahora acepta sus responsabilidades y demuestra interés y entusiasmo por la escuela.

◆ _____'s attitude is improving since he/she has developed a greater interest in his/her schoolwork. He/she now seems eager to learn.

❖ La actitud de _____ está mejorando, pues demuestra mayor interés en sus tareas. Ahora parece tener entusiasmo por aprender.

◆ I am happy to report that I have seen considerable improvement in _____'s attitude.

❖ Me alegra informar que he visto considerable mejora en la actitud de _____ .

Attitude

Needs Improvement (Necesita Mejorar)

◆ ___ often lacks motivation. If he/she improved his/her classroom attitude and applied more effort, his/her grades would also improve.

❖ _____ a menudo no tiene motivación. Si mejorara su actitud en el salón de clases e hiciera un mayor esfuerzo, sus calificaciones mejorarían.

◆ _____ requires a lot supervision. His/her disruptive nature interferes with his/her learning. Please encourage him/her to act more responsibly and develop a better attitude toward school.

❖ _____ necesita mucha supervisión. Su tendencia a la indisciplina interfiere con su aprendizaje. Por favor motivenlo(a) para que se comporte con más responsabilidad y mejore su actitud hacia la escuela.

◆ _____ can be very helpful and dependable in the classroom. However, he/she does not always have a good attitude about completing assignments. Please encourage him/her to be more positive about this important aspect of learning.

❖ _____ puede ser un buen colaborador(a) y dedicado(a) en el salón de clases. Sin embargo, no siempre muestra una buena actitud para hacer sus tareas. Por favor motivenlo(a) para que sea más positivo(a) con este aspecto del aprendizaje.

Behavior

Proficient (Competente)

- ◆ _____ is a good citizen. He/she is dependable, responsible, and respectful.
- ❖ _____ es un(a) buen(a) ciudadano(a). Muestra tener dedicación, responsabilidad y respeto.

- ◆ _____ shares and listens. He/she works well with others.
- ❖ _____ sabe compartir y escuchar. Trabaja bien con otros.

- ◆ _____ is a pleasant, respectful, and well-behaved student.
- ❖ _____ es un(a) estudiante respetuoso(a), de personalidad agradable y de buen comportamiento.

Making Progress (Está Progresando)

- ◆ Since our last conference, _____'s behavior has been improving. He/she is showing an interest in his/her schoolwork and seems eager to learn.
- ❖ Desde nuestra última reunión, el comportamiento de _____ ha mejorado. Muestra interés en sus tareas y parece tener entusiasmo por aprender.

- ◆ _____ is showing an increased desire to demonstrate appropriate attitude and acceptable behavior in the classroom.
- ❖ _____ muestra mayor interés por demostrar una actitud apropiada y un comportamiento aceptable en el salón de clases.

- ◆ _____ is learning to anticipate the consequences of his/her actions. This is improving his/her behavior because he/she is taking time to think before acting.
- ❖ _____ está aprendiendo a prever las consecuencias de sus actos. Esto ha mejorado su comportamiento, ya que piensa antes de actuar.

- ◆ _____ is learning to react in more socially appropriate ways. Consequently, he/she is making more friends.
- ❖ _____ está aprendiendo a reaccionar de manera más sociable. En consecuencia, está haciendo más amistades.

- ◆ There has been noticeable improvement in _____'s behavior. He/she has made an effort to cooperate with his/her peers and practice self control. Thank you for your support.
- ❖ El comportamiento de _____ ha mejorado notablemente. Ha hecho un esfuerzo para colaborar con sus compañeros y controlarse. Muchas gracias por su apoyo.

Behavior

Making Progress (Está Progresando) *(cont.)*

◆ Lately _____ has been working to correct his/her behavior, and I am very proud of him/her. I hope he/she continues to maintain this improvement.

❖ Últimamente, _____ se esfuerza por corregir su comportamiento y eso me llena de satisfacción. Espero que siga así.

Needs Improvement (Necesita Mejorar)

◆ _____ is very aggressive towards his classmates. Perhaps we should have him/her meet with the school counselor.

❖ _____ es muy agresivo(a) con sus compañeros. Quizás debería tener una reunión con el consejero escolar.

◆ Please encourage _____ to use socially appropriate language at all times.

❖ Por favor motiven a _____ para que use lenguaje socialmente apropiado en todo momento.

◆ Socializing is more important to _____ than classwork. He/she has great potential, but will not realize it until he/she pays better attention in class and focuses more on his/her work.

❖ Para _____ , relacionarse con los demás es más importante que las tareas escolares. Tiene grandes aptitudes, pero para desarrollarlas, debe poner más atención en clase y concentrarse más en sus tareas.

◆ _____ can be very disruptive and disorderly. Please encourage him/her to be more responsible in his/her behavior, and call me to schedule a conference.

❖ _____ a veces tiene un comportamiento revoltoso y desordenado. Por favor motivenlo(a) para que tenga un comportamiento más responsable y que se comuniquen conmigo para programar una reunión.

Effort

Proficient (Competente)

◆ _____ uses his/her time wisely. He/she is working to full capacity in all subjects.

❖ _____ usa muy bien su tiempo Está aplicando toda su capacidad en todas las asignaturas.

◆ _____ is highly motivated to do his/her personal best. He/she is a joy to teach!

❖ _____ muestra gran motivación para dar lo mejor de sí. ¡Es un placer enseñarle!

◆ _____ is enthusiastic about work and performs well in everything he/she undertakes.

❖ _____ muestra entusiasmo por sus tareas y le va muy bien en todo lo que hace.

◆ _____ is a hard worker. With his/her ability to apply himself/herself, _____ should be successful throughout his/her school career.

❖ _____ muestra gran dedicación. Si sigue usando esta capacidad de trabajo, toda su carrera escolar será un éxito.

Making Progress (Está Progresando)

◆ _____ is becoming more dependable during work periods. His/her work has improved steadily.

❖ _____ muestra más dedicación en los períodos de trabajo. Sus tareas mejoran continuamente.

◆ _____ has made a great effort to improve in his/her schoolwork.

❖ _____ ha hecho un gran esfuerzo por mejorar sus tareas.

◆ _____ has shown an encouraging desire to improve. He/she is making steady progress. Your encouragement is appreciated.

❖ _____ ha demostrado un alentador deseo de mejorar y progresa continuamente. Muchas gracias por motivarlo(a).

◆ If _____ will put forth the effort he/she has shown this past grading period, he/she should be on grade level by the end of the year.

❖ Si _____ sigue haciendo el esfuerzo que ha demostrado en el último período de evaluación, al final del año alcanzará el nivel del grado.

◆ _____ is now demonstrating responsibility by beginning and completing tasks without needing frequent reminders.

❖ _____ está demostrando responsabilidad. Comienza y realiza las tareas sin necesidad de que se lo recuerden a menudo.

Effort

Needs Improvement (Necesita Mejorar)

◆ _____'s schoolwork is inconsistent and does not always reflect his/her ability. If he/she put forth more effort, _____ could work to his/her ability and improve the quality of his/her work.

❖ El rendimiento de _____ no es consistente y no siempre refleja su capacidad. Si hace más esfuerzo, _____ podría usar toda su capacidad y mejorar la calidad de sus tareas.

◆ _____ does not complete assignments in the allotted time. He/she needs to apply more effort and learn to pace himself/herself.

❖ _____ no realiza sus tareas en el tiempo asignado. Necesita hacer más esfuerzo y aprender a regular su ritmo de trabajo.

◆ In order for _____ to be successful in school, he/she will need to take responsibility for his/her own work and apply himself/herself to each task.

❖ Para que a _____ le vaya bien en la escuela, necesitará hacerse responsable de sus tareas y dedicarse a ellas.

◆ _____ needs encouragement and direct supervision to apply effort to his/her work. I would like to schedule a conference to discuss _____'s progress.

❖ _____ necesita motivación y supervisión directa para que dedique esfuerzo a sus tareas. Me gustaría que programáramos una reunión para hablar del avance de _____ .

Outdoor Behavior

Proficient (Competente)

◆ _____ is very athletic and shows good sportsmanship. Everyone enjoys playing with him/her outside.

❖ _____ muestra buenas condiciones atléticas y espíritu deportivo. A todos sus compañeros les gusta jugar con él/ella.

◆ _____ is a leader on the playground. He/she influences others to make wise choices, organizes games, and invites others to play.

❖ _____ es líder en el patio de juegos. Influye en otros para que tomen buenas decisiones, organiza juegos e invita a jugar a los demás.

◆ _____ enjoys physical activity. He/she uses the playground equipment appropriately and shows good sportsmanship.

❖ A _____ le gustan las actividades físicas. Hace buen uso del equipamiento del patio de juegos y muestra buen espíritu deportivo.

Making Progress (Está Progresando)

◆ _____'s behavior is improving outside. He/she is making better choices and trying to follow the rules.

❖ El comportamiento de _____ fuera del salón de clases está mejorando. Toma mejores decisiones y trata de seguir las reglas.

◆ _____ is involved in fewer incidences on the playground. We review outdoor rules every day, and this seems to be making a difference.

❖ _____ tiene menos incidentes en el patio de juegos. Repasamos las reglas del patio todos los días y esto parece haber ayudado.

◆ _____ is showing more self-control outside. He/she is beginning to respect the personal space of other students.

❖ _____ muestra más autocontrol fuera del salón de clases. Comienza a respetar el espacio personal de los demás estudiantes.

Outdoor Behavior

Needs Improvement (Necesita Mejorar)

◆ _____ works well in the classroom. However, during outside times, he/she finds it difficult to join groups.

❖ _____ trabaja muy bien en el salón de clases. Sin embargo, fuera de él le cuesta integrarse en los grupos.

◆ _____ is having trouble on the playground. The duty personnel report that he/she is disrespectful and uncooperative. We need to work together to help _____ accept and respect the authority of the adults supervising the playground.

❖ _____ tiene dificultades en el patio de juegos. Los supervisores de turno informan que es irrespetuoso(a) y poco colaborador(a). Es necesario que trabajemos juntos para ayudar a que _____ acepte y respete la autoridad de los adultos que supervisan el patio de juegos.

◆ Occasionally, _____ has problems outside. This affects his/her classroom demeanor and ability to learn. Please discuss this matter with him/her.

❖ A veces, _____ tiene problemas fuera del salón de clases. Esto afecta su comportamiento en clase y su capacidad de aprender. Es conveniente que ustedes hablen de esto con él/ella.

Self-Confidence

Proficient (Competente)

◆ _____ is a very happy, well-adjusted child. He/she speaks with confidence in a group.

❖ _____ es un(a) niño(a) muy alegre y equilibrado(a). Habla con seguridad en un grupo.

◆ _____ is very confident. He/she makes friends easily and is well-liked by his/her classmates.

❖ _____ muestra mucha seguridad en sí mismo(a). Hace amigos con facilidad y es muy popular entre sus compañeros.

◆ _____ participates in class and is willing to take risks. This reflects in his/her academic performance.

❖ _____ participa en clase y no teme asumir riesgos. Esto se refleja en su rendimiento académico.

Making Progress (Está Progresando)

◆ _____ is gaining more self-confidence. He/she is beginning to grow in independence.

❖ _____ muestra más seguridad en sí mismo(a). Comienza a ser más independiente.

◆ _____ is a conscientious student. He/she is gaining independence, but still needs frequent encouragement.

❖ _____ es un(a) estudiante aplicado(a). Muestra más independencia, pero aún necesita motivación frecuente.

◆ _____ has matured nicely. There is a noticeable improvement in his/her self-confidence, and he/she is now willing to take more risks.

❖ _____ ha madurado muy bien. Esto es una notable mejoría para la seguridad en sí mismo(a) y ahora muestra más disposición para asumir riesgos.

Self-Confidence

Needs Improvement (Necesita Mejorar)

◆ _____ is anxious to please others. He/she copies others and hesitates to make independent decisions. Please encourage _____ to be more independent, even if he/she makes some mistakes.

❖ A _____ le interesa mucho agradar a los demás. Copia lo que hacen los otros y duda en tomar decisiones propias. Por favor motivenlo para que sea más independiente, aunque a veces se equivoque.

◆ _____ needs a lot of reassurance. He/she gets upset easily and sometimes cries. We need to work on developing his/her confidence so he/she can become more self-reliant.

❖ _____ necesita que lo(a) tranquilicen muy a menudo. Se altera con facilidad y a veces llora. Necesitamos trabajar para desarrollar su seguridad y para que logre más independencia.

◆ _____ hesitates to participate and is unwilling to take risks. This is affecting his/her academic performance. We need to persuade him/her to take small risks, then larger ones. During this period of development, we will need to offer _____ encouragement and support.

❖ _____ duda en participar y no muestra disposición para asumir riesgos. Esto afecta su rendimiento académico. Es necesario convencerlo(a) de que comience a asumir pequeños riesgos primero y luego riesgos más grandes. Durante este período de desarrollo, debemos darle motivación y apoyo a _____ .

Social Skills

Proficient (Competente)

◆ _____ has a pleasant personality. He/she is learning to share, cooperate, and be fair. _____ is a great addition to our classroom!

❖ _____ tiene una agradable personalidad. Está aprendiendo a compartir, cooperar y actuar con justicia. _____ es una valiosa incorporación a nuestro salón de clases.

◆ _____ always has time to do something nice for other students. For this reason, he/she is well-liked among his/her peers.

❖ _____ siempre encuentra tiempo para hacer algo bueno por otros estudiantes. Por esa razón es muy popular entre sus compañeros.

◆ _____ is cheerful and friendly. He/she assumes responsibility, excels in the classroom, and is well-liked by his/her peers.

❖ _____ es alegre y cordial. Asume sus responsabilidades, se destaca en el salón de clases y es muy popular entre sus compañeros.

◆ _____ shows initiative. He/she thinks things through and goes the extra mile on all assignments.

❖ _____ demuestra tener iniciativa. Piensa muy bien las cosas y pone dedicación adicional en todas sus tareas.

Making Progress (Está Progresando)

◆ _____'s social maturity is improving. We need to continue supporting him/her in this area.

❖ La madurez social de _____ está mejorando. Es necesario que sigamos apoyándolo(a) en esta área.

◆ _____ is well-liked by his/her peers now that he/she is being friendly and helpful to others.

❖ _____ es muy popular entre sus compañeros. Ahora es cordial y colaborador(a) con los demás.

◆ I am pleased with the progress that _____ is making. He/she has become more cooperative and is learning to work well in groups.

❖ Me alegra ver el avance de _____ . Es más colaborador(a) y está aprendiendo a trabajar bien en grupo.

◆ _____ has a great sense of humor that we all enjoy. He/she is now learning when it is more appropriate to be serious.

❖ _____ tiene un muy buen sentido del humor que todos disfrutamos. Ahora está aprendiendo cuándo es más apropiado ser serio(a).

Social Skills

Needs Improvement (Necesita Mejorar)

◆ _____ frequently interrupts others. We will be working to develop patience.

❖ _____ a menudo interrumpe a los demás. Trabajaremos para desarrollar su paciencia.

◆ _____ tries to dominate every activity. He/she needs to take turns and be more considerate of others.

❖ _____ trata de dominar cada actividad. Debe esperar su turno y ser más considerado con los demás.

◆ _____ has a pleasant personality, but he/she talks constantly. This is affecting his/her academic performance and that of others. Please encourage him/her to be more respectful of his/her learning time and that of others.

❖ _____ tiene una agradable personalidad, pero habla constantemente. Esto afecta su rendimiento académico y el de los demás. Es conveniente que ustedes lo(a) motiven para que respete más su tiempo de aprendizaje y el de los demás.

◆ _____ is quite reserved around the other students. If possible, provide more opportunities for interaction with peers through a small religious group or other kinds of social groups. Hopefully, this additional contact will help him/her feel more comfortable with other students.

❖ _____ es bastante reservado(a) con sus compañeros. Si es posible, denle más oportunidades para relacionarse con otros niños en algún pequeño grupo religioso o de otro tipo. Es de esperar que este contacto adicional lo(a) ayude a sentirse más cómodo(a) con otros estudiantes.

Work Habits

Proficient (Competente)

- ◆ _____ is a hard worker and occupies his/her time constructively.
- ❖ _____ muestra gran dedicación y usa su tiempo de manera constructiva.

- ◆ _____ is working to his/her full potential. He/she is organized and thorough in his/her work.
- ❖ _____ está aplicando todas sus aptitudes. Su trabajo muestra organización y esmero.

- ◆ _____ works independently on assignments. He/she demonstrates great organizational skills.
- ❖ _____ hace sus tareas en forma independiente. Demuestra excelentes destrezas de organización.

- ◆ _____ has good organization of thoughts. He/she is a good student who appears to be a deep thinker.
- ❖ _____ organiza muy bien las ideas. Es un(a) buen(a) estudiante que parece pensar las cosas con profundidad.

- ◆ _____ is a good worker and an attentive listener; he/she is a delight!
- ❖ _____ muestra gran dedicación y escucha con mucha atención. Es un gran placer trabajar con él/ella.

Making Progress (Está Progresando)

- ◆ _____ is learning to use his/her time constructively. Thank you for talking to him/her about this concern.
- ❖ _____ está aprendiendo a usar el tiempo de manera constructiva. Muchas gracias por hablar con él/ella de este tema.

- ◆ Since our last conference, _____ is taking more pride in his/her work. Thank you for your support.
- ❖ Desde nuestra última reunión, _____ toma sus tareas más en serio. Muchas gracias por su apoyo.

Work Habits

Making Progress (Está Progresando) *(cont.)*

◆ _____ is beginning to listen more carefully and follow directions. I am expecting continued growth in this area.

❖ _____ comienza a escuchar con más atención y a seguir instrucciones. Espero que siga progresando en esta área.

◆ Rather than depending on others, _____ now utilizes a variety of resources to complete his/her assignments.

❖ En lugar de depender de otros, _____ ahora usa diferentes recursos para hacer sus tareas.

Needs Improvement (Necesita Mejorar)

◆ _____ needs to concentrate more fully on his/her own work and not be distracted by his/her neighbors. This would result in better work habits and more learning.

❖ _____ necesita concentrarse más en sus tareas y no distraerse con sus compañeros. Esto mejoraría su aprendizaje y sus hábitos de trabajo.

◆ Please encourage _____ to take more care as he/she completes his/her work. It is often disorganized.

❖ Por favor motiven a _____ para que ponga más cuidado cuando hace sus tareas. A menudo son desorganizadas.

◆ _____ has a lot of potential, but he/she must improve his/her work habits in order to gain the fundamentals needed for _____ grade work.

❖ _____ tiene muchas aptitudes, pero debe mejorar sus hábitos de trabajo para alcanzar el nivel necesario de _____ grado.

◆ Please encourage _____ to focus on his/her work and complete assignments in the allotted time.

❖ Por favor motiven a _____ para que se concentre en sus trabajos y las haga en el tiempo asignado.

General Messages

Most report card comments focus on academic performance and behavior. However, there are other situations and circumstances that require pertinent observations. A new student's arrival, a homework problem, or a decision about a student's retention may prompt the need for relevant comments.

The General Messages section addresses these and a variety of other situations. Although the headings and comments in this section do not duplicate previous areas, they do overlap them.

Our largest category is devoted to year-end messages. These final comments are extremely important because they summarize the student's progress for the entire year. They often convey a message about what is most important about a student. Year-end comments can reflect the teacher's concern for the student. They can also become part of a lasting record, since the final report card is often saved.

Consequently, final comments should be as positive and hopeful as possible without sending a false message. When improvement is needed, comments should be tactfully phrased to encourage progress. The year-end messages in this section include positive, concise statements, as well as constructive comments that suggest a means to realize potential. To facilitate your use of this category, we have once again used the labels of "Proficient," "Making Progress," and "Needs Improvement."

Homework

Proficient (Competente)

◆ _____ consistently completes his/her homework. His/her preparation for class is superior.

❖ _____ siempre completa sus tareas en la casa. Su preparación para la clase es sobresaliente.

◆ I appreciate the way _____ completes homework assignments. His/her work is neat and always on time.

❖ Aprecio la forma en que _____ hace su tarea. Su trabajo es organizado y siempre puntual.

◆ _____'s homework is always completed carefully and thoughtfully. He/she should be commended for such effort.

❖ _____ siempre hace su tarea con atención y esmero. Merece felicitaciones por su esfuerzo.

Making Progress (Está Progresando)

◆ _____ has taken more care on his/her homework. It is now neat and accurate.

❖ _____ pone más cuidado en sus tareas. Ahora son organizadas y correctas.

◆ I can tell that _____ is devoting more effort to his/her homework. It is more accurate and his/her test scores are improving.

❖ Observo que _____ dedica más esfuerzo a sus tareas. Ahora son más precisas y las calificaciones de sus exámenes están mejorando.

◆ Since _____ has been doing extra homework, he/she has improved in all areas. It is great to see him/her striving to meet his/her potential.

❖ Desde que _____ hace tareas extras, ha mejorado en todas las áreas. Es muy bueno ver que se esfuerza para desarrollar sus aptitudes.

Homework

Making Progress (Está Progresando) *(cont.)*

◆ _____ now turns in his/her homework about 80% of the time.   This is a great improvement. Let's work toward 100%!

❖ _____ ahora entrega sus tareas un 80% de las veces. Esto es un gran avance. ¡Ahora busquemos el 100%!

Needs Improvement (Necesita Mejorar)

◆ _____ needs to put more effort into his/her homework. He/she meets all deadlines, but should be encouraged to improve the quality of his/her work.

❖ _____ necesita poner más esfuerzo en sus tareas. Las entrega siempre a tiempo, pero hay que motivarlo(a) para que mejore la calidad de su trabajo.

◆ _____ needs to give more attention to his/her homework. It should be completed with more care and turned in on time.

❖ _____ necesita poner más atención a sus tareas. Debe poner más cuidado en ellas y entregarlas a tiempo.

◆ _____ does not hand in all of his/her homework. He/she is missing _____ assignments. Please talk to him/her about the importance of returning homework.

❖ _____ no entrega todas sus tareas. Le faltan _____ tareas. Es conveniente que ustedes hablen con él/ella sobre la importancia de entregar las tareas.

◆ _____ has not adequately prepared for our tests. He/she needs to complete his/her homework every day.

❖ _____ no tiene la preparación adecuada para sus exámenes. Debe hacer sus tareas todos los días.

◆ _____ received makeup homework when he/she was absent. The homework was not returned, and this has affected his/her grade. Please have her/him complete and return it.

❖ A _____ se le asignaron tareas extras por su ausencia. No entregó estas tareas y esto influye en su calificación. Por favor haganlo(a) completar y entregar sus tareas.

New Student

Proficient (Competente)

◆ Although _____ has been in our class for just a short time, he/she has made a great adjustment. The other students enjoy working with him/her, and he/she has made a lot of friends. We are glad he/she joined our class!

❖ Aunque hace poco que _____ está en nuestra clase, se ha adaptado muy bien. Ha hecho muchas amistades y a los demás estudiantes les gusta trabajar con él/ella. ¡Nos alegra que esté en nuestra clase!

◆ _____ fits in very well in our classroom. He/she has made a good adjustment both socially and academically since he/she joined our class.

❖ Desde que _____ se incorporó a nuestra clase, se adaptó muy bien, tanto social como académicamente.

◆ I am so pleased that _____ has moved into our classroom. He/she is a delight!

❖ Me alegra mucho que _____ se haya incorporado a nuestro salón de clases. Es un placer trabajar con él/ella.

Making Progress (Está Progresando)

◆ _____ is more adjusted to our class now. He/she seems to understand the work better, and he/she has made some good friends.

❖ _____ se ha adaptado mejor a nuestra clase. Parece entender mejor las tareas y ha hecho algunos buenos amigos.

◆ _____ did not seem to enjoy our class during his/her first few weeks here, but I am seeing an improvement now. I think he/she will feel even more comfortable in a few more weeks.

❖ Aparentemente, durante las primera semanas, a _____ no le gustaba nuestra clase, pero ahora observo un avance. Creo que se sentirá aún mejor en unas semanas.

◆ _____ made friends quickly, but struggled academically during his/her first month in our class. He/she has been steadily improving.

❖ _____ hizo amigos muy rápidamente. Aunque durante el primer mes de clases tuvo dificultades académicas, ha mejorado en forma constante.

New Student

Needs Improvement (Necesita Mejorar)

◆ Since joining our class, _____ has struggled both academically and socially. He/she fights on the playground, and this problem is carrying over into the classroom. Please call for a conference.

❖ Desde que se incorporó a nuestra clase, _____ ha tenido dificultades académicamente y socialmente. Se pelea en el patio de juegos y este problema se traslada al salón de clases. Les ruego se comuniquen conmigo para programar una reunión.

◆ _____ interacts well with the other students. However, he/she is having problems adjusting to the structure of our classroom. Please come in so we can discuss how to help him/her.

❖ _____ se relaciona bien con los demás estudiantes. Sin embargo, está teniendo dificultades para adaptarse a la estructura del salón de clases. Es conveniente que ustedes vengan a la escuela para que hablemos sobre cómo podemos ayudarlo(a).

◆ _____ has made a lot of friends since he/she joined our class, but he/she is struggling with the schoolwork. We need to schedule a conference to discuss the curriculum and his/her progress at his/her previous school.

❖ Desde que se incorporó a nuestra clase, _____ ha hecho muchas amistades, aunque tiene dificultades con sus tareas. Es necesario que programemos una reunión para hablar del plan de estudios y de su avance en la escuela anterior.

Above Average Student

- ◆ _____ has an excellent attitude. He/she adds to the learning atmosphere in our class.

- ❖ _____ demuestra una excelente actitud. Contribuye a la atmósfera de aprendizaje de nuestra clase.

- ◆ _____ uses his/her class time wisely; he/she makes good decisions.

- ❖ _____ usa muy bien su tiempo de clase y toma buenas decisiones.

- ◆ _____ is working above grade level. His/her achievement is outstanding!

- ❖ _____ está trabajando por encima del nivel de este grado. ¡Su rendimiento es sobresaliente!

- ◆ _____ is an excellent student. He/she has worked hard and excels in all subjects.

- ❖ _____ es un(a) estudiante excelente. Ha trabajado con gran dedicación y se destaca en todas las asignaturas.

- ◆ You should be very proud of _____ . He/she is a conscientious student and is always trying to improve his/her skills.

- ❖ Ustedes deben estar muy orgullosos de _____ . Es un(a) estudiante aplicado(a) y siempre trata de mejorar sus destrezas.

- ◆ I can always depend on _____ to set a good example for the rest of the students. It is a pleasure having him/her in my class.

- ❖ Siempre puedo confiar que _____ dará un buen ejemplo al resto de los estudiantes. Es un placer que esté en mi clase.

- ◆ I have enjoyed having _____ in my class. He/she always makes pertinent and interesting contributions to our class discussions.

- ❖ Ha sido un placer tener a _____ en mi clase. Siempre hace comentarios adecuados y interesantes durante las discusiónes de clase.

Above Average Student

◆ _____ completes his/her work quickly and accurately. He/she is cooperative and attentive. He/she is a delight!

❖ _____ hace sus tareas de manera rápida y correcta. Colabora y pone atención en clase. Es un placer trabajar con él/ella.

◆ _____ is gifted; he/she is my top student and can tackle challenges in any academic area.

❖ _____ tiene mucho talento. Es mi mejor estudiante y puede sortear desafíos en todas las áreas académicas.

◆ _____ is very bright. He/she seeks out new information and learning and consistently challenges himself/herself.

❖ _____ es muy inteligente. Busca nueva información y aprender más. Constantemente busca desafíos para sí.

◆ _____ is a very capable student, but does not like challenges because he/she does not like to fail.

❖ _____ es muy capaz, pero no le gustan los desafíos porque no le gusta fallar.

◆ _____ is a very bright student, but does not work to his/her potential. He/she needs to seek out new learning and challenge himself/herself.

❖ _____ es muy inteligente, pero no aplica todas sus aptitudes. Debe intentar aprender más y encontrar desafíos para él/ella.

◆ _____ is an excellent student. However, he/she is too competitive; he/she always has to be first and is unhappy if he/she doesn't win. This has become a problem in our class. Please discuss this at home.

❖ _____ es un(a) estudiante excelente. Sin embargo, es demasiado competitivo(a). Siempre quiere estar en primer puesto y si no lo logra, se siente mal. Esto se ha convertido en un problema en nuestra clase. Es conveniente que ustedes hablen de esto con él/ella en su casa.

Average Student

◆ _____ participates in all of our class activities. The effort he/she applies to his/her work is commendable.

❖ _____ participa en todas las actividades de la clase. Su esfuerzo es muy meritorio.

◆ _____ displays good study skills and works well in a group. He/she shows great interest in our studies and takes pride in his/her work.

❖ _____ tiene buenas destrezas de estudio y trabaja bien en un grupo. Muestra gran interés en nuestros estudios y toma sus tareas muy en serio.

◆ _____ is performing at grade level. His/her daily work is very good.

❖ El rendimiento de _____ está en el nivel de este grado. Su trabajo diario es muy bueno.

◆ _____ is showing satisfactory progress in his/her schoolwork.

❖ _____ muestra un avance satisfactorio en sus tareas.

◆ _____ has been working very hard at school. His/her efforts are making a difference. Please encourage him/her to continue.

❖ _____ ha mostrado gran dedicación en la escuela. Sus esfuerzos han dado fruto. Por favor motivenlo(a) a seguir así.

◆ _____ has a lot of potential, however, his/her socializing inhibits his/her progress. He/she could improve his/her grades by focusing on his/her work.

❖ _____ tiene muchas aptitudes. Sin embargo, sus interacciones con los compañeros afectan su progreso. Si se concentra en sus tareas, podría mejorar sus calificaciones.

◆ _____ is a dedicated worker and always does his/her best. He/she is having trouble understanding _____ . Please help him/her complete the enclosed work pages.

❖ _____ muestra gran dedicación y siempre pone su mayor esfuerzo. Tiene dificultades para entender _____ . Por favor ayudenlo(a) a que haga las tareas adjuntas.

Average Student

- ◆ _____ has done a good job on his/her (math, reading, writing), however, he/she still struggles with _____ . He/she would benefit from some extra help at home.

- ❖ _____ ha obtenido buenos resultados en (matemáticas, lectura, redacción). Sin embargo, sigue teniendo dificultades con _____ . Se beneficiaría con ayuda extra en su casa.

- ◆ _____ is showing satisfactory progress in all areas. Thank you for encouraging him/her at home.

- ❖ _____ muestra avances satisfactorios en todas las áreas. Muchas gracias por motivarlo(a) en casa.

- ◆ I am pleased with the progress that _____ has made. The extra work you are doing at home is making a difference. Please continue _____ .

- ❖ Me alegra ver el avance de _____ . El trabajo extra que está haciendo en su casa ha sido de gran ayuda. Por favor sigan _____ .

- ◆ I have enjoyed having _____ in my room. He/she is a willing worker with a high interest in everything that we do.

- ❖ Ha sido un placer tener a _____ en mi clase. Muestra una excelente disposición para trabajar y un gran interés por todo lo que hacemos.

- ◆ _____ is a cooperative student and an active participant in our class. His/her basic skills are strong, and he/she is working at grade level.

- ❖ _____ es muy buen(a) colaborador(a) y participa activamente en nuestra clase. Tiene sólidas destrezas básicas y está trabajando en el nivel de este grado.

- ◆ _____ is doing satisfactory work; he/she should easily be ready for _____ grade by the end of the year.

- ❖ _____ está trabajando de manera satisfactoria. Fácilmente alcanzará la preparación necesaria para el _____ grado a fin de año.

Below Average Student

- ◆ In order to improve the quality of his/her work, _____ needs to complete it with more care. He/she also needs to ask for help when he/she struggles with an assignment.

- ❖ Para mejorar la calidad de sus tareas, _____ necesita poner más atención cuando las hace. También debe pedir ayuda cuando tiene dificultades con una tarea.

- ◆ _____ does not use his/her time effectively, and he/she often daydreams. When he/she learns to pay more attention in class and focus on his/her work, he/she will be more successful.

- ❖ _____ no usa su tiempo con eficacia y a menudo se distrae, pensando en otra cosa. Para mejorar su rendimiento, necesita aprender a poner más atención en clase y a concentrarse en sus tareas.

- ◆ _____ needs to develop better organizational skills and study habits. He/she needs to take daily notes and set aside time to study them.

- ❖ _____ necesita desarrollar mejores destrezas de organización y hábitos de estudio. Debe tomar notas todos los días y dedicar tiempo para estudiarlas.

- ◆ _____'s last test scores were low. I will let him/her retake the test on _____ . Please help him/her study at home.

- ❖ Las calificaciones del último examen de _____ fueron bajas. Le pediré que vuelva a tomar el examen en _____ . Por favor ayudenlo(a) a estudiar en su casa.

- ◆ _____'s test scores are low, and he/she does not follow directions. We need to schedule a conference to discuss possible solutions.

- ❖ Las calificaciones de los exámenes de _____ son bajas y no sigue las instrucciones. Es necesario que programemos una reunión para hablar de posibles soluciones.

- ◆ _____ needs to participate in discussions and work to his/her potential.

- ❖ Es necesario que _____ participe en las discusiónes y aplique todas sus aptitudes.

- ◆ _____ has not made enough progress since our last conference. When he/she makes more effort, his/her grades will improve.

- ❖ _____ no ha tenido suficiente avance desde nuestra última reunión. Si se esfuerza más, sus calificaciones mejorarán.

- ◆ Thank you for coming to conference with me. Our conversation has helped me understand _____ better. Although he/she is struggling, I think our plan will help him/her make progress.

- ❖ Muchas gracias por haber venido a la reunión. Nuestra conversación me ayudó a entender mejor a _____ . Aunque está teniendo dificultades, creo que nuestro plan ayudará a su progreso.

Below Average Student

◆ _____ is always willing to help. Although the work is difficult for him/her, he/she tries everything. Please continue helping him/her at home.

❖ _____ siempre muestra disposición para ayudar. Aunque se le dificultan las tareas, lo intenta todo. Por favor sigan ayudándolo(a) en su casa.

◆ _____'s work is below grade level. He/she needs to concentrate and develop better study habits.

❖ El rendimiento de _____ está por debajo del nivel de este grado. Debe concentrarse y desarrollar mejores hábitos de estudio.

◆ I am concerned about _____'s progress. His/her work habits and command of the basic subjects are below grade level. Please help him/her complete all homework assignments.

❖ Me preocupa el nivel de avance de _____ . Sus hábitos de trabajo y su dominio de temas básicos están por debajo del nivel de este grado. Por favor ayudenlo(a) a hacer todas las tareas.

◆ _____ tries hard to please, however, he/she is struggling in school. We need to discuss a plan of action. Please call me for a conference.

❖ _____ hace un gran esfuerzo, pero tiene dificultades en la escuela. Es necesario que elaboremos un plan de acción. Les ruego se comuniquen conmigo para programar una reunión.

Retention

- ◆ As you requested, _____ will repeat the _____ grade. I agree that the extra time will be beneficial to him/her.

- ❖ Como lo solicitaron, _____ repetirá el _____ grado. Estoy de acuerdo que ese tiempo adicional lo(a) beneficiará.

- ◆ _____'s scores are low, and I do not feel he/she will be successful in _____ grade. We need to meet and discuss his/her placement for next year.

- ❖ Las calificaciones de _____ son bajas. Lamentablemente, no creo que esté preparado(a) para el _____ grado. Es necesario que nos reunamos para hablar de su ubicación el año próximo.

- ◆ I am considering _____ for retention this year. It is imperative that he/she come to school every day prepared and ready to learn.

- ❖ Creo que quizás _____ debería repetir el grado. Es indispensable que venga a la escuela todos los días, preparado(a) y dispuesto(a) a aprender.

- ◆ Because of your child's late summer birthday, he/she is not ready for _____ grade. He/she needs another year to mature. As we discussed at our last conference, repeating this grade is in the best interest of your child.

- ❖ Debido a que su hijo(a) cumple años a final del verano, no está preparado(a) para el _____ grado. Necesita otro año para poder madurar. Como lo conversamos en nuestra última reunión, repetir el grado es lo que más beneficiará a su hijo(a).

Retention

◆ _____ is a delightful child, but he/she is performing below grade level. Although, he/she is starting to make progress, another year in this grade would greatly benefit him/her.

❖ _____ es un(a) niño(a) maravilloso(a), pero su rendimiento está por debajo del nivel de este grado. Aunque comenzó a progresar, otro año en este grado será un gran beneficio para él/ella.

◆ I have enjoyed working with _____ this year. He/she has made progress, but is not ready for the rigors of _____ grade. Another year in _____ grade will help strengthen his/her academic foundation.

❖ Ha sido un placer trabajar con _____ este año. Lamentablemente, aunque ha progresado, no está preparado(a) para las exigencias del _____ grado. Otro año en el _____ grado lo(a) ayudará a tener una base académica más sólida.

◆ _____ is slowly improving in all academic areas. However, he/she is not yet working at grade level. I am concerned whether he/she will be ready for _____ grade by the end of the year. Let's talk about his/her placement in another month.

❖ Aunque _____ está mejorando lentamente en todas las áreas académicas, aún no tiene el nivel de este grado. Me preocupa que pueda no estar preparado(a) para el _____ grado a fin de año. Hablemos de su ubicación dentro de un mes.

◆ Although _____ is ready for _____ grade in most areas, he/she will need to continue the _____ grade reading program until it is completed. He/she will receive additional support next year to ensure success.

❖ Aunque _____ está preparado(a) para el _____ grado en la mayoría de las áreas, deberá continuar el program de lectura del _____ grado hasta terminarlo. Recibirá ayuda adicional el año próximo para asegurar un buen resultado.

◆ I am happy to report that since _____ was retained last year, he/she has blossomed. He/she has more confidence and is working at grade level.

❖ Me alegra informar que desde que _____ repitió el año anterior, ha mejorado. Muestra más seguridad y está trabajando en el nivel de este grado.

Year-End Messages

Proficient (Competente)

◆ It was a pleasure to have _____ in class. He/she is a conscientious worker, as well as a thoughtful, considerate classmate.

❖ Fue un placer tener a _____ en clase. Muestra gran dedicación en sus tareas y gran consideración por sus compañeros.

◆ It has been a joy to teach _____ ! He/she is reading easily at a _____ grade level. I expect great things from him/her in the future!

❖ ¡Ha sido un placer enseñarle a _____! Lee perfectamente en el nivel de _____ grado. ¡Espero grandes cosas de él/ella en el futuro!

◆ I have loved being _____'s teacher! He/she is a wonderful student who makes teaching a joy! Thank you for letting me be a part of his/her education. I expect great things from him/her in the future!

❖ ¡Ha sido un placer enseñarle a _____! Ha sido un(a) estudiante maravilloso. Muchas gracias por permitirme participar en su educación. ¡Espero grandes cosas de él/ella en el futuro!

◆ I enjoyed having _____ in my class. He/she demonstrates leadership, accepts responsibility, and takes pride in his/her work.

❖ Ha sido un placer tener a _____ en mi clase. Demuestra cualidades de liderazgo, asume responsabilidades y toma sus tareas muy en serio.

◆ It has been a joy to teach _____ ! I will miss his/her enthusiasm and great smile. He/she has made amazing progress this year. I expect great things from him/her!

❖ ¡Ha sido un placer enseñarle a _____ ! Extrañaré su gran entusiasmo y su linda sonrisa. Ha tenido un avance asombroso este año. ¡Espero grandes cosas de él/ella en el futuro!

◆ _____ has been a joy to teach! He/she has made amazing progress and is ready for _____ grade. Thank you for the privilege of being his/her teacher.

❖ ¡Ha sido un placer enseñarle a _____ ! Ha tenido un avance asombroso y está preparado(a) para el _____ grado. Muchas gracias por permitirme el privilegio de enseñarle.

◆ _____ is a model student; he/she is bright, dedicated, and self-disciplined. Thank you for the opportunity to teach such a delightful child!

❖ _____ es un(a) estudiante modelo. Es inteligente, dedicado(a) y disciplinado(a). ¡Muchas gracias por permitirme la oportunidad de enseñarle a un(a) niño(a) tan maravilloso(a)!

Year-End Messages

Proficient (Competente) *(cont.)*

- ◆ It has been a joy to teach _____; he/she is so full of wonder and personality! He/she has made great progress this year in all areas.

- ❖ Ha sido un placer enseñarle a _____. ¡Es un(a) niño(a) maravilloso(a) de gran personalidad! Ha tenido un avance excelente en todas las áreas.

- ◆ I have enjoyed teaching _____ . He/she is a smart girl/boy who is ready for _____ grade. He/she is also a class leader with many friends. Enjoy your summer with him/her!

- ❖ Ha sido un placer enseñarle a _____. Es un(a) niño(a) muy inteligente y está preparado(a) para el _____ grado. También es líder en la clase y tiene muchos amigos. ¡Que disfruten del verano en su compañía!

- ◆ _____ has been a joy to teach! He/she has worked very hard and made great progress this year. He/she has a natural curiosity and a great desire to learn! Best of luck in _____ grade.

- ❖ Ha sido un placer enseñarle a _____. Ha trabajado con gran dedicación y ha tenido un excelente progreso este año. ¡Tiene una curiosidad natural y muchos deseos de aprender! Mucha suerte en el _____ grado.

- ◆ I have truly enjoyed teaching _____ ; he/she is a reflection of great parents. _____ made great academic progress and is ready to advance. I will miss the _____ family!

- ❖ Ha sido un verdadero placer enseñarle a _____. Es un reflejo de unos padres maravillosos. _____ tuvo un excelente avance académico y está preparado(a) para avanzar. ¡Extrañaré esta familia!

- ◆ It was a pleasure to teach _____ this year. He/she is cooperative, courteous, and considerate of others.

- ❖ Ha sido un placer enseñarle a _____ este año. Es colaborador(a), cortés y considerado(a) con los demás.

- ◆ I have loved teaching _____ . He/she has been an eager learner and an active participant in all that we have done. He/she should not have any trouble in _____ grade.

- ❖ Ha sido un placer enseñarle a _____. Ha mostrado interés por aprender y ha participado activamente en todo lo que hemos hecho. Seguramente no tendrá dificultades en el _____ grado.

Year-End Messages

Proficient (Competente) *(cont.)*

- ❖ I have enjoyed having _____ in class. He/she works diligently and gets along with the other students. His/her _____ skills are solid, and he/she is reading at a _____ grade level.

- ❖ Ha sido un placer tener a _____ en mi clase. Ha trabajado con gran dedicación y se lleva bien con los demás estudiantes. Tiene sólidas destrezas de _____ y lee en el nivel del _____ grado.

- ❖ _____ accomplished a lot this year; his/her skills are strong and he/she is reading fluently. He/she is an active participant in the learning process. _____ is a joy to teach!

- ❖ _____ tuvo muchos logros este año. Tiene sólidas destrezas y lee con fluidez. Participa activamente en el proceso de aprendizaje. ¡Es un placer enseñarle a _____ !

- ❖ I am glad _____ was in my class. His/her academic skills are strong, and he/she has the potential for developing strong leadership skills. He/she is a great student!

- ❖ Ha sido un placer tener a _____ en mi clase. Tiene sólidas destrezas académicas y excelentes destrezas de liderazgo. ¡Es muy buen(a) estudiante!

- ❖ _____ is ready for any challenge. He/she is reading _____ grade material and working above grade level in many areas. _____ is friendly, outgoing, and enthusiastic. I have enjoyed being his/her teacher!

- ❖ _____ está preparado(a) para cualquier desafío. Está leyendo material de _____ grado y trabajando por encima del nivel de su grado en muchas áreas. Es cordial, extrovertido(a) y entusiasta. ¡Ha sido un placer enseñarle!

- ❖ _____ is an extraordinary girl/boy. He/she participates in all activities and works well with the other students. _____ made great progress and should enjoy _____ grade. I have enjoyed being his/her teacher!

- ❖ _____ es un(a) niño(a) extraordinario(a). Participa en todas las actividades y trabaja bien con los demás estudiantes. _____ tuvo un gran avance y seguramente disfrutará del _____ grado. ¡Ha sido un placer enseñarle!

- ❖ _____ has strong academic skills. He/she is working above grade level in all areas.

- ❖ _____ tiene sólidas destrezas académicas. Está trabajando por encima del nivel de este grado en todas las áreas.

- ❖ _____ is popular, helpful, and ready for anything! I am glad he/she was in my class.

- ❖ _____ es popular, colaborador(a) y está preparado(a) para todo. Ha sido un placer tenerlo(a) en mi clase.

Year-End Messages

Proficient (Competente) *(cont.)*

◆ _____ has been a lot of fun this year. He/she has a love of learning that is pushing him/her to the top of the class. He/she has been an asset to our classroom.

❖ La presencia de _____ este año ha sido muy productiva para el salón de clases y la hemos disfrutado. A _____ le gusta mucho aprender, lo cual le permitió llegar a ser el/la mejor de la clase.

◆ It has been a pleasure to have _____ in class this year. With his/her continued effort and excellence, he/she will receive much satisfaction.

❖ Ha sido un placer tener a _____ en clase este año. Con su continuado esfuerzo y excelencia, tendrá muchas satisfacciones.

◆ _____ has made this a pleasant year. His/her progress has been impressive! Thank you for your support and interest. Have a wonderful summer!

❖ _____ ha hecho que este año sea muy lindo. ¡Su progreso ha sido admirable! Muchas gracias a ustedes por la ayuda y el interés. ¡Que tengan un maravilloso verano!

◆ I enjoyed having _____ in class. He/she has a great sense of humor and gets along well with his/her peers. I have high expectations for him/her in the future.

❖ Ha sido un placer tener a _____ en mi clase. Tiene muy buen sentido del humor y se lleva bien con sus compañeros. Espero grandes cosas de él/ella en el futuro.

◆ _____ has been a wonderful addition to our class! He/she has been a friendly, cooperative, and enthusiastic learner.

❖ ¡_____ ha sido una contribución maravillosa para nuestra clase! Ha sido un(a) estudiante cordial, colaborador(a) y entusiasta.

◆ _____ has made great progress this year. His/her effort in our class was impressive! I hope this attitude and effort will carry over to the next school year.

❖ _____ ha tenido un excelente avance este año. ¡Su esfuerzo en nuestra clase fue asombroso! Confío en que conserve la misma actitud y esfuerzo el próximo año escolar.

◆ _____ is a conscientious student who should have much success in school. His/her friendly, sincere way has made him/her very popular. It has been a pleasure to have him/her in my class.

❖ _____ es un(a) estudiante aplicado(a) que seguramente tendrá excelentes resultados en la escuela. Su cordialidad y sinceridad lo(a) hicieron muy popular. Ha sido un placer tenerlo(a) en mi clase.

Year-End Messages

Proficient (Competente) *(cont.)*

- ◆ _____ has been a fine citizen and a constant contributor. I am sure he/she will be very successful next year.

- ❖ _____ ha sido un(a) ciudadano(a) responsable y un(a) constante colaborador(a). Tengo la seguridad de que tendrá excelentes resultados el año próximo.

- ◆ _____ takes pride in his/her work; it is always neat and thorough. His/her work habits are impressive and his skills are strong. I have enjoyed being his/her teacher.

- ❖ _____ toma sus tareas muy en serio. Siempre son ordenadas y correctas. Tiene admirables hábitos de trabajo y sólidas destrezas. Ha sido un placer enseñarle.

- ◆ _____ has earned a fine report card this semester. He/she is cooperative, happy, and a good citizen. _____ is a dedicated student, and I expect him/her to excel in _____ grade.

- ❖ Este semestre, la boleta de calificaciones de _____ fue excelente. Es colaborador(a), alegre, un(a) ciudadano(a) responsable y un(a) estudiante dedicado(a). Confío en que se destacará en el _____ grado.

- ◆ _____ made steady progress in all areas this year. He/she is definitely ready for _____ grade. _____ has a high interest in learning. I have enjoyed being his/her teacher.

- ❖ _____ ha tenido un progreso constante en todas las áreas este año. Definitivamente, está preparado(a) para el _____ grado. _____ muestra un gran interés por aprender. Ha sido un placer enseñarle.

- ◆ _____ is a delightful boy/girl. He/she has strong skills in all areas. _____ is enthusiastic about learning. I have loved being his/her teacher.

- ❖ _____ es un(a) niño(a) maravilloso(a). Tiene sólidas destrezas en todas las áreas y gran entusiasmo por aprender. Ha sido un placer enseñarle.

Making Progress (Está Progresando)

- ◆ It has been a treat to have _____ in my classroom. There has been a noticeable improvement in his/her work. With continued effort, he/she will have great success in school.

- ❖ Ha sido un placer tener a _____ en mi salón de clases. Ha mostrado un avance notable en sus tareas. Si sigue esforzándose, tendrá excelentes resultados en la escuela.

Year-End Messages

Making Progress (Está Progresando) *(cont.)*

◆ _____ is a fine citizen and a hard worker. I have enjoyed watching him/her blossom this year. With continued effort, he/she should do well in school.

❖ _____ es un(a) ciudadano(a) responsable y de gran dedicación. Ha sido un placer ver cómo progresó este año. Si sigue esforzándose, tendrá muy buenos resultados en la escuela.

◆ _____ has done well in school. Practice his/her skills this summer to keep him/her prepared for _____ grade. It has been a joy to teach _____ ; he/she has a great personality!

❖ A _____ le ha ido muy bien en la escuela. Si practica sus destrezas en el verano, seguirá preparado(a) para el _____ grado. Ha sido un placer enseñarle. ¡Tiene una gran personalidad!

◆ I have loved teaching _____ . He/she has worked diligently, made great progress, and is ready for _____ grade.

❖ Ha sido un placer enseñarle a _____ . Ha trabajado con gran dedicación, ha tenido un avance excelente y está preparado(a) para el _____ grado.

◆ _____ has matured nicely this year. He/she takes an interest in his/her work and always does his/her personal best.

❖ _____ ha madurado bastante este año. Se interesa en sus tareas y siempre da lo mejor de sí.

◆ _____ has made wonderful academic progress and is well on his/her way to reading. It has been a joy to be his/her teacher!

❖ _____ ha tenido un maravilloso avance académico y está aprendiendo a leer muy bien. ¡Ha sido un placer enseñarle!

◆ _____ is a great student! I have truly enjoyed being his/her teacher. He/she has worked very hard and made great progress. With continued support, he/she should do well in _____ grade.

❖ ¡_____ es muy buen(a) estudiante! Ha sido un verdadero placer enseñarle. Ha trabajado con gran dedicación y ha tenido un excelente avance. Con ayuda constante, le irá muy bien en el _____ grado.

◆ _____ is now at grade level! He/she needs to practice this summer to keep his/her skills sharp. I have loved being his/her teacher.

❖ _____ logró el nivel de este grado. Debe practicar en el verano para mantener sus destrezas. Ha sido un placer enseñarle.

Year-End Messages

Making Progress (Está Progresando) *(cont.)*

- ◆ _____ is always eager to help his/her classmates; he/she has the potential to be a leader. _____ has improved steadily throughout the year. It has been a privilege to teach him/her.

- ❖ _____ siempre está dispuesto(a) a ayudar a sus compañeros(as) y tiene aptitudes de líder. _____ ha mejorado continuamente durante el año. Ha sido un privilegio enseñarle.

- ◆ _____ made continual progress this year. His/her interest in our classroom activities steadily increased; at the same time his/her skills improved. Thank you for helping at home.

- ❖ _____ tuvo avances constantes este año. Su interés en las actividades del salón de clases aumentaron de manera continua. Al mismo tiempo, sus destrezas mejoraron. Muchas gracias por su ayuda en casa.

- ◆ _____ has had to work at every stage, but he/she has been willing to put forth the effort. He/she is on grade level, but continue practicing _____ this summer to maintain skills. _____ is a great student!

- ❖ _____ tuvo que esforzarse en cada etapa, pero ha mostrado voluntad para el trabajo. Está en el nivel del grado, pero debe seguir practicando _____ este verano para mantener sus destrezas. ¡_____ es un(a) gran estudiante!

Year-End Messages

Needs Improvement (Necesita Mejorar)

◆ I enjoyed teaching _____ . He/she made a lot of improvement this year, but is still working below grade level. The class requirements will need to be modified again next year.

❖ Ha sido un placer enseñarle a _____. Ha mejorado mucho este año, pero sigue trabajando por debajo del nivel de este grado. Los requisitos de la clase deberán modificarse nuevamente el año próximo.

◆ _____ is a delightful girl/boy. He/she made a lot of improvement, but needs to practice reading every day this summer. Please continue reviewing math skills also. I have enjoyed being his/her teacher; good luck in _____ grade.

❖ _____ es un(a) niño(a) maravilloso(a). Ha mejorado mucho, pero debe practicar la lectura todos los días este verano. También necesita seguir repasando las destrezas de matemáticas. Ha sido un placer enseñarle. Mucha suerte en el _____ grado.

◆ In order for _____ to be ready for _____ grade this fall, please continue to practice and review skills at home. I have enclosed a packet of summer homework that highlights the skills that still need to be mastered.

❖ Para que _____ esté preparado(a) para el _____ grado este otoño, debe seguir practicando y repasando sus destrezas en su casa. Adjunto un paquete de tareas para el verano, que destacan las destrezas que deben dominarse.

◆ I am afraid that _____ is going to struggle in _____ grade. Although his/her academic skills are at grade level, he/she has had a difficult time behaving. This is going to affect his/her learning as well as distract the rest of the class. Please try some of the strategies we have used throughout the year to reinforce better behavior.

❖ Temo que _____ necesitará hacer un esfuerzo en el _____ grado. Aunque sus destrezas académicas están en el nivel del grado, le ha costado comportarse. Esto afectará su aprendizaje y además distraerá al resto de la clase. Conviene usar en su casa algunas de las estrategias que utilizamos durante el año para reforzar el buen comportamiento.

Words and Phrases

After choosing comments from this book, you may want to extend some of them. The Words and Phrases section serves as an excellent resource for augmenting report card comments.

As you complete a comment for a student, facts and examples can be added to substantiate it. By selecting words or phrases that are most appropriate, you can develop a comment that accurately and specifically describes a student or situation.

The lists in the Words and Phrases section can assist you in personalizing your comments. You can use the same reading comment for a number of students, then individualize each with a different set of words or phrases.

The Words and Phrases section can also inspire and guide you as you write your own comments. The suggested words can help you effectively create comments that are interesting and meaningful.

To facilitate the use of this section, the lists are divided into the following categories:

- Academics
- Attitude
- Behavior
- Communication
- Connecting with Families
- Creativity
- General
- Helpful Adjectives
- Helpful Verbs
- Two-Word Phrases
- Work Habits

Academics

Proficient (Competente)

- ◆ I am excited to see progress in _____
- ❖ Me entusiasma ver su avance en _____

- ◆ demonstrates depth and insight in writing
- ❖ demuestra profundidad y agudeza en redacción

- ◆ I am trying to help _____ by _____
- ❖ Estoy tratando de ayudar a _____ al _____

- ◆ _____ is a high achiever
- ❖ _____ logra sus metas

- ◆ demonstrates a high level of competence
- ❖ demuestra una gran capacidad

- ◆ utilizes successful strategies
- ❖ usa buenas estrategias

- ◆ greatly skilled in _____
- ❖ tiene excelentes destrezas de _____

- ◆ methodical in solving problems
- ❖ metódico(a) para resolver problemas

- ◆ excels in analytical thinking
- ❖ se destaca en pensamiento analítico

- ◆ concentrates on analyzing facts
- ❖ se concentra en el análisis de datos

- ◆ is working well in all subjects
- ❖ trabaja bien en todas las asignaturas

- ◆ greatly skilled in _____
- ❖ tiene excelentes destrezas de _____

Academics

Proficient (Competente) *(cont.)*

◆ demonstrates a high level of expertise

❖ demuestra gran conocimiento

◆ possesses high expertise in _____

❖ tiene gran conocimiento de _____

◆ excels in assisting others with _____

❖ se destaca en ayudar a los demás en _____

◆ displays a high sense of inquiry

❖ demuestra un gran sentido para la investigación

◆ displays a strong power of observation

❖ demuestra un gran poder de observación

◆ completes projects with impressive results

❖ hace trabajos con resultados asombrosos

◆ contributes thoughtful comments to _____ discussions

❖ aporta comentarios reflexivos a discusiónes de _____

◆ capable of reading demanding texts

❖ capaz de leer textos difíciles

◆ chooses to read during free time

❖ elige leer en su tiempo libre

◆ willingly takes suggestions from peers and teacher

❖ acepta con gusto las sugerencias de compañeros y maestros

◆ self-edits during the writing process

❖ corrige su propio trabajo en el proceso de redacción

◆ produces highly accurate work

❖ produce tareas muy correctas

Academics

Making Progress (Está Progresando)

- ◆ working harder now to meet academic goals
- ❖ trabaja con más dedicación ahora para alcanzar las metas académicas

- ◆ makes better use of resources
- ❖ hace un mejor uso de los recursos

- ◆ more fully prepared
- ❖ mejor preparado(a)

- ◆ is developing correct capitalization and punctuation
- ❖ está aprendiendo a usar las mayúsculas y los signos de puntuación correctamente

- ◆ now requires a minimum of guidance when completing assignments
- ❖ ahora necesita un mínimo de orientación para hacer sus tareas

- ◆ continuously strives to strengthen _____
- ❖ constantemente trabaja para reforzar _____

- ◆ continuously strives to improve performance
- ❖ constantemente trabaja para mejorar su rendimiento

- ◆ is now organizing work well
- ❖ ahora organiza muy bien su trabajo

- ◆ is more orderly and systematic
- ❖ es más ordenado(a) y metódico(a)

Academics

Needs Improvement (Necesita Mejorar)

- ◆ with greater effort, he/she can improve his/her _____
- ❖ con más esfuerzo, puede mejorar su _____

- ◆ as he/she continues to mature academically, _____ will experience greater success
- ❖ si sigue madurando académicamente, _____ tendrá mejores resultados

- ◆ thinking outside of the box is a challenge
- ❖ tener ideas originales es un desafío

- ◆ needs to develop stronger skills in _____
- ❖ necesita desarrollar destrezas más sólidas en _____

- ◆ needs to be encouraged to take risks in writing
- ❖ necesita motivación para que se atreva a asumir riesgos en redacción

- ◆ needs strengthening in _____ skills
- ❖ necesita reforzar sus destrezas de _____

- ◆ struggling to understand the concepts of _____
- ❖ tiene dificultades para entender los conceptos de _____

- ◆ could exceed grade level goals with greater effort
- ❖ con un mayor esfuerzo, podría superar las metas de nivel del grado

- ◆ needs to be encouraged to read
- ❖ necesita motivación para que lea

- ◆ needs help using reference books
- ❖ necesita ayuda para usar libros de referencia

- ◆ needs to be encouraged to successfully complete all assignments
- ❖ necesita motivación para hacer todas las tareas en forma exitosa

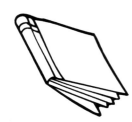

- ◆ is not working to his/her potential
- ❖ no está aplicando todas sus aptitudes

Connecting with Families

◆ we need to schedule a conference

❖ es necesario que programemos una reunión

◆ please call for an appointment

❖ les ruego se comuniquen conmigo para hacer una cita

◆ feel free to call for an appointment

❖ no duden en comunicarse conmigo para hacer una cita

◆ thank you for your help

❖ muchas gracias por su ayuda

◆ I appreciate your willingness to help

❖ aprecio su disposición para ayudar

◆ I appreciate your support

❖ aprecio la ayuda de ustedes

◆ thank you for practicing daily on _____ at home

❖ gracias por practicar _____ diariamente en su casa

◆ please encourage your child to _____

❖ por favor alienten a su hijo(a) para que _____

◆ thank you for volunteering to help in our class

❖ muchas gracias por ofrecerse voluntariamente a ayudar en nuestra clase

◆ your continual support has helped _____ improve in _____

❖ el continuo apoyo de ustedes ha ayudado a que _____ mejore en _____

Connecting with Families

◆ has benefited from consistent parent-teacher communication

❖ se ha beneficiado con la permanente comunicación entre padres y maestros

◆ looking forward to seeing you at our learning night

❖ espero verlos en nuestra noche de aprendizaje

◆ please call if you have questions or concerns

❖ les ruego se comuniquen conmigo si tienen preguntas o inquietudes

◆ thank you for being a partner in _____'s education

❖ muchas gracias por colaborar en la educación de _____

◆ your help is greatly appreciated

❖ agradezco profundamente la ayuda de ustedes

◆ glad you were able to attend the parent night

❖ me alegró que pudieran asistir a la noche para padres

◆ your help has benefited everyone in our classroom

❖ la ayuda de ustedes ha beneficiado a todos en nuestro salón de clases

Work Habits

Proficient (Competente)

- ◆ demonstrates a high level of independence
- ❖ demuestra una gran independencia

- ◆ his/her excellent work is a reflection of his/her effort
- ❖ su excelente trabajo es un reflejo de su esfuerzo

- ◆ seeks out highly challenging tasks
- ❖ busca tareas muy desafiantes

- ◆ outstanding organizational skills
- ❖ sobresalientes destrezas de organización

- ◆ displays good study skills
- ❖ demuestra buenas destrezas de estudio

- ◆ displays a strong sense of priorities
- ❖ demuestra gran capacidad para fijar prioridades

- ◆ uses time wisely
- ❖ usa muy bien su tiempo

- ◆ recognizes the importance of accuracy
- ❖ reconoce la importancia de la exactitud

- ◆ strives for perfection
- ❖ busca la perfección

- ◆ meticulous with details
- ❖ detallista

- ◆ makes effective use of _____
- ❖ hace un uso eficaz de _____

- ◆ effectively uses technology
- ❖ usa la tecnología con eficacia

- ◆ shows maximum effort
- ❖ demuestra un máximo esfuerzo

Work Habits

Proficient (Competente) *(cont.)*

◆ excels in self-pacing

❖ se destaca en la regulación de su ritmo de trabajo

◆ motivated to achieve high standards

❖ motivado(a) para lograr un buen nivel

◆ displays an enthusiastic spirit

❖ demuestra un espíritu entusiasta

◆ displays an intense desire

❖ demuestra un intenso deseo

◆ goes beyond what is expected

❖ va más allá de lo que se espera

◆ is totally absorbed in school

❖ está totalmente concentrado(a) en la escuela

◆ is success-oriented

❖ persigue el éxito

◆ is not content with mediocrity

❖ no le gusta la mediocridad

◆ works well with others

❖ trabaja bien con otros

◆ plans appropriate strategies to arrive at solutions

❖ planea estrategias adecuadas para encontrar soluciones

◆ takes initiative in solving problems

❖ tiene iniciativa para resolver problemas

◆ anticipates opportunities

❖ prevé las oportunidades

◆ develops positive strategies

❖ desarrolla estrategias positivas

Work Habits

Making Progress (Está Progresando)

◆ should be encouraged to _____

❖ debe motivársele para que _____

◆ is learning to listen carefully

❖ está aprendiendo a escuchar con atención

◆ _____'s determination and effort have raised his/her grades

❖ la decisión y el esfuerzo de _____ han mejorado sus calificaciones

◆ is working toward becoming conscientious in completing his/her work

❖ trabaja para ser más aplicado(a) en la realización de sus tareas

◆ is gaining independence in _____

❖ se está haciendo más independiente en _____

◆ displays a willingness to make improvements

❖ muestra disposición para mejorar

◆ is better at sustaining concentration now

❖ ahora tiene mayor concentración

◆ now gives maximum effort

❖ ahora pone su esfuerzo máximo

◆ is more task-oriented

❖ muestra más disposición para hacer tareas

◆ is completing tasks in an efficient manner now

❖ ahora hace sus tareas con más eficiencia

◆ now capable of assuming greater responsibility

❖ ahora es capaz de asumir mayores responsabilidades

Needs Improvement (Necesita Mejorar)

◆ rarely participates in discussions

❖ rara vez participa en discusiónes

Work Habits

Needs Improvement (Necesita Mejorar) *(cont.)*

◆ needs continual guidance and supervision

❖ necesita continua orientación y supervisión

◆ needs highly-structured directions

❖ necesita instrucciones muy estructuradas

◆ _____ 's note-taking needs improvement

❖ _____ necesita aprender a tomar mejores notas

◆ needs to take pride in his/her work

❖ necesita tomar sus tareas más en serio

◆ does not complete assignments on time

❖ no hace sus tareas puntualmente

◆ needs to concentrate on his/her own work

❖ necesita concentrarse en sus tareas

◆ needs to learn to contribute in a more appropriate manner

❖ necesita aprender a contribuir de manera más adecuada

◆ constantly seeks teacher assistance

❖ busca constantemente la ayuda del maestro/de la maestra

◆ needs more consistent practice

❖ necesita más práctica constante

◆ excessive tardies and absences

❖ demasiadas llegadas tardes y ausencias

◆ encourage him/her to strive for quality work

❖ motívenlo(a) para que mejore la calidad de sus tareas

◆ needs to complete assignments with more care

❖ necesita poner más cuidado al hacer sus tareas

◆ is inclined to be dependent on others for directions

❖ tiende a depender de las instrucciones de los demás

General

Proficient (Competente)

- ◆ impresses me with his/her focus
- ❖ me impresiona su concentración

- ◆ is a pleasure to have _____ in class
- ❖ es un placer tener a _____ en mi clase

- ◆ a creative problem solver
- ❖ creativo(a) para resolver problemas

- ◆ makes fine contributions to our class
- ❖ hace excelentes aportes a nuestra clase

- ◆ is intuitive
- ❖ es intuitivo(a)

- ◆ continues to amaze me with his/her insights
- ❖ siempre me asombra con su perspicacia

- ◆ is very compassionate
- ❖ es muy compasivo(a)

- ◆ conscientious, hardworking student
- ❖ estudiante aplicado(a) y trabajador(a)

- ◆ has a wonderful sense of humor
- ❖ tiene un maravilloso sentido del humor

- ◆ is friendly and cooperative
- ❖ es amigable y colaborador(a)

- ◆ is well-spoken
- ❖ habla con corrección y educación

- ◆ is well-liked by his/her classmates
- ❖ es popular entre sus compañeros

- ◆ demonstrates incredible leadership skills
- ❖ demuestra sorprendentes destrezas de liderazgo

General

Proficient (Competente) *(cont.)*

- ◆ has blossomed this year
- ❖ ha mejorado este año

- ◆ bubbles over with enthusiasm
- ❖ tiene muchísimo entusiasmo

- ◆ an energetic participant in all activities
- ❖ un(a) estudiante que participa con gran energía en todas las actividades

- ◆ is dependable in carrying out responsibilities
- ❖ asume sus responsabilidades

- ◆ displays diligence in performing tasks
- ❖ es aplicado(a) en el cumplimiento de sus tareas

- ◆ can be relied upon
- ❖ es digno(a) de confianza

- ◆ displays a strong commitment to successfully completing projects
- ❖ se dedica seriamente a realizar sus trabajos

- ◆ displays a strong capacity for growth
- ❖ demuestra gran capacidad de crecimiento

- ◆ has a great deal of energy and enthusiasm
- ❖ tiene mucha energía y entusiasmo

- ◆ always makes time to assist others
- ❖ siempre encuentra tiempo para ayudar a los demás

- ◆ is a joy to have _____ in class
- ❖ es un placer tener a _____ en mi clase

- ◆ always willing to give extra effort
- ❖ siempre muestra disposición para esforzarse más

- ◆ benefits from constructive criticism
- ❖ aprovecha la crítica constructiva

General

Proficient (Competente) *(cont.)*

- ◆ sets ambitious goals
- ❖ fija metas ambiciosas

- ◆ is a self-starter
- ❖ toma iniciativas

- ◆ takes initiative in solving problems
- ❖ tiene iniciativa para resolver problemas

- ◆ seizes all opportunities
- ❖ aprovecha todas las oportunidades

- ◆ plans and organizes with little or no assistance
- ❖ planea y organiza con poca o ninguna ayuda

- ◆ demonstrates innovative insight
- ❖ demuestra perspicacia innovadora

- ◆ makes a favorable impression
- ❖ causa una impresión favorable

- ◆ is accepted by others
- ❖ tiene aceptación entre los demás

- ◆ establishes effective working relationships
- ❖ establece relaciones eficaces de trabajo

- ◆ promotes harmony among classmates
- ❖ promueve la armonía entre los compañeros

- ◆ exercises considerable influence within the group
- ❖ tiene considerable influencia en el grupo

- ◆ interacts effectively with peers
- ❖ se relaciona bien con sus compañeros

- ◆ clearly understands objectives and procedures
- ❖ entiende con claridad los objetivos y procedimientos

General

Proficient (Competente) *(cont.)*

◆ is exceptionally well-informed

❖ está excepcionalmente bien informado(a)

◆ projects enthusiasm and self-confidence

❖ muestra entusiasmo y seguridad en sí mismo(a)

◆ displays an exceptional ability to learn

❖ demuestra una excepcional capacidad de aprender

◆ is totally committed to achieving excellence

❖ está totalmente dedicado(a) a lograr la excelencia

◆ works with enthusiasm

❖ trabaja con entusiasmo

◆ is able to overcome extreme difficulties

❖ es capaz de superar dificultades extremas

◆ is task-oriented

❖ muestra disposición para hacer tareas

◆ ambitious and high-spirited

❖ ambicioso(a) y alegre

◆ displays a pleasant, cheerful disposition

❖ demuestra una disposición agradable y alegre

◆ possesses all traits associated with excellence

❖ tiene todas las características asociadas con la excelencia

◆ displays a pleasing personality

❖ tiene una personalidad agradable

◆ has an outgoing personality

❖ tiene una personalidad extrovertida

◆ brings a fresh perspective into our classroom

❖ aporta una visión renovada a nuestro salón de clases

General

Making Progress (Está Progresando)

- ◆ is more reliable now when given an assignment
- ❖ ahora cumple más con sus tareas

- ◆ could profit by _____
- ❖ podría beneficiarse al _____

- ◆ is beginning to blossom in all areas
- ❖ comienza a mejorar en todas las áreas

- ◆ developing a sense of responsibility towards his/her learning
- ❖ desarrolla un sentido de responsabilidad en su proceso de aprendizaje

- ◆ shows improvement in making contributions to class projects
- ❖ muestra que está mejorando en sus contribuciones a trabajos de clase

- ◆ displays a willingness to make improvements
- ❖ muestra disposición para mejorar

- ◆ uses suggestions to improve performance
- ❖ aplica las sugerencias para mejorar su rendimiento

- ◆ displays an eagerness to improve
- ❖ demuestra deseos de mejorar

- ◆ shows steady progress
- ❖ muestra un progreso constante

- ◆ continues to grow and improve
- ❖ sigue creciendo y mejorando

- ◆ demonstrates an ability to relate to his/her classmates
- ❖ demuestra capacidad para relacionarse con sus compañeros

- ◆ demonstrates a better understanding of procedures
- ❖ demuestra que entiende mejor los procedimientos

General

Making Progress (Está Progresando) *(cont.)*

- ◆ is showing more leadership skills
- ❖ muestra más destrezas de liderazgo

- ◆ is more receptive to new ideas
- ❖ está más abierto(a) a nuevas ideas

- ◆ is beginning to grasp new routines
- ❖ comienza a adoptar nuevas rutinas

- ◆ is showing more effort to maintain skills
- ❖ muestra más esfuerzo para mantener destrezas

- ◆ displays a renewed sense of purpose
- ❖ muestra tener nuevas metas

- ◆ is now demonstrating independent thinking
- ❖ ahora demuestra pensamiento independiente

- ◆ is displaying a stronger commitment to _____
- ❖ está demostrando un compromiso más sólido con _____

- ◆ projects more energy and enthusiasm
- ❖ muestra más energía y entusiasmo

Needs Improvement (Necesita Mejorar)

- ◆ should be encouraged to _____
- ❖ debe motivársele para que _____

- ◆ needs to accept responsibility for his/her actions
- ❖ necesita asumir la responsabilidad de sus actos

- ◆ has difficulty with _____
- ❖ se le dificulta _____

- ◆ appears inattentive
- ❖ parece distraído(a)

General

Needs Improvement (Necesita Mejorar) *(cont.)*

- ◆ takes action too hastily
- ❖ actúa precipitadamente

- ◆ needs constant reassurance
- ❖ necesita aprobación constante

- ◆ needs to be more open-minded
- ❖ necesita tener una actitud más abierta

- ◆ needs more hands-on experiences
- ❖ necesita más experiencias prácticas

- ◆ relies too heavily on others
- ❖ depende demasiado de los demás

- ◆ emulates peers instead of making independent decisions
- ❖ en lugar de tomar decisiones propias, copia a los demás

- ◆ needs encouragement to achieve potential
- ❖ necesita motivación para desarrollar sus aptitudes

- ◆ shows little enthusiasm for learning
- ❖ muestra poco entusiasmo por aprender

- ◆ needs to learn from mistakes
- ❖ necesita aprender de los errores

- ◆ needs to take pride in his/her work
- ❖ necesita tomar sus tareas en serio

- ◆ needs to be encouraged to use common sense
- ❖ necesita motivación para que use el sentido común

- ◆ would improve performance with more study
- ❖ mejoraría su rendimiento si estudiara más

- ◆ needs encouragement to develop leadership skills
- ❖ necesita motivación para desarrollar sus destrezas de liderazgo

Behavior

Proficient (Competente)

- ◆ demonstrates good judgment
- ❖ demuestra tener buen criterio

- ◆ promotes cooperative behavior and team effort
- ❖ promueve el comportamiento colaborador y el trabajo de equipo

- ◆ is conscientious
- ❖ es aplicado(a)

- ◆ is an involved learner
- ❖ es un(a) estudiante que participa

- ◆ cooperates with his/her peers
- ❖ colabora con sus compañeros

- ◆ displays a high degree of integrity
- ❖ demuestra una gran integridad

- ◆ exhibits a high degree of emotional maturity
- ❖ muestra una gran madurez emocional

- ◆ presents different opinions without creating conflicts
- ❖ da opiniones diferentes sin crear conflictos

- ◆ handles confrontations with tact
- ❖ maneja las confrontaciones con tacto

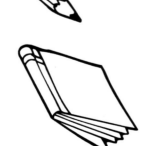

- ◆ is very cordial/polite
- ❖ es muy cordial/educado(a)

- ◆ is sincere
- ❖ es sincero(a)

- ◆ excels in developing "what if" scenarios
- ❖ se destaca en la elaboración de situaciones hipotéticas

Behavior

Proficient (Competente) *(cont.)*

- ◆ always has a smile on his/her face
- ❖ está siempre sonriente

- ◆ greatly focused on work
- ❖ muy concentrado(a) en sus tareas

- ◆ is a class leader
- ❖ es líder de la clase

- ◆ is a determined learner
- ❖ es un(a) estudiante con decisión

- ◆ is a dependable student
- ❖ es un(a) estudiante digno(a) de confianza

- ◆ demonstrates empathy toward his/her classmates
- ❖ demuestra que entiende a sus compañeros

Making Progress (Está Progresando)

- ◆ is beginning to be responsible for staying on task
- ❖ comienza a asumir la responsabilidad de concentrarse en un trabajo

- ◆ participates more fully when monitored by the teacher
- ❖ participa más activamente cuando su maestro(a) lo(a) supervisa

- ◆ has become more cooperative
- ❖ ahora es más colaborador(a)

- ◆ is now maintaining attention to the task at hand
- ❖ ahora mantiene la atención en la tarea que está haciendo

- ◆ is making wiser choices
- ❖ ahora toma mejores decisiones

Behavior

Making Progress (Está Progresando) *(cont.)*

- ◆ much improved behavior
- ❖ comportamiento ha mejorado muchisimo

- ◆ is becoming more self-reliant
- ❖ comienza a ser más independiente

- ◆ keeps anger under better control
- ❖ controla mejor la ira

- ◆ is becoming more flexible
- ❖ comienza a ser más flexible

- ◆ is beginning to participate more
- ❖ comienza a participar más

- ◆ is showing more consideration for others' feelings
- ❖ ahora muestra más consideración por los sentimientos de los demás

- ◆ is becoming more patient
- ❖ está aprendiendo a ser más paciente

- ◆ is more focused on work
- ❖ se concentra más en sus tareas

- ◆ is developing leadership skills
- ❖ está desarrollando destrezas de liderazgo

- ◆ requires less teacher supervision during independent work time
- ❖ requiere menos supervisión de su maestro(a) en los momentos de trabajo independiente

Behavior

Needs Improvement (Necesita Mejorar)

- ◆ manages his/her peers too much
- ❖ dirige demasiado a sus compañeros

- ◆ his/her socialization inhibits academic progress
- ❖ sus interacciones con los compañeros afectan su progreso académico

- ◆ finds it difficult to make a smooth transition between activities
- ❖ tiene dificultades para cambiar de actividad con fluidez

- ◆ needs to display a more cooperative nature
- ❖ debe mostrar una disposición más colaboradora

- ◆ needs to develop a calmer temperament
- ❖ necesita desarrollar un temperamento más tranquilo

- ◆ follows school rules only when closely monitored
- ❖ sigue las reglas de la escuela sólo cuando se le supervisa de cerca

- ◆ has difficulty following directions
- ❖ tiene dificultades para seguir instrucciones

- ◆ needs to develop self-control
- ❖ necesita aprender a controlarse

- ◆ is showing minimal improvement since our last grading period
- ❖ muestra una mejoría mínima desde el período de evaluación anterior

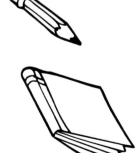

- ◆ requires a lot of supervision
- ❖ requiere mucha supervisión

- ◆ avoids emotional involvement
- ❖ evita involucrarse emocionalmente

Behavior

Needs Improvement (Necesita Mejorar) *(cont.)*

- ◆ needs to cope constructively with emotions
- ❖ necesita aprender a manejar sus emociones de manera constructiva

- ◆ needs to think before taking action
- ❖ necesita aprender a pensar antes de actuar

- ◆ needs to know appropriate times to speak
- ❖ necesita reconocer el momento adecuado para hablar

- ◆ needs to take responsibility for his/her actions
- ❖ necesita asumir la responsabilidad de sus actos

- ◆ requires guidance and supervision to minimize disruptive behavior
- ❖ requiere orientación y supervisión para superar su indisciplina

- ◆ has trouble functioning in group settings
- ❖ tiene dificultades para participar en grupos

- ◆ needs to use humor constructively
- ❖ necesita aprender a usar el humor de manera constructiva

- ◆ capable of assuming a greater leadership role
- ❖ capaz de asumir un mayor rol de liderazgo

- ◆ successful within a consistent structure
- ❖ exitoso(a) en una estructura firme

- ◆ is challenged during work time by his/her social nature
- ❖ se ve desafiado(a) por su naturaleza sociable durante el tiempo de trabajar

Communication

Proficient (Competente)

- ◆ communicates clearly and concisely
- ❖ se comunica con claridad y síntesis

- ◆ excels in interpersonal communications
- ❖ se destaca en la comunicación con los demás

- ◆ asks pertinent questions
- ❖ hace preguntas adecuadas

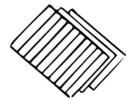

- ◆ listens carefully
- ❖ escucha con atención

- ◆ effectively communicates ideas
- ❖ comunica ideas con eficacia

- ◆ effectively explains and interprets _____
- ❖ explica e interpreta _____ con eficacia

- ◆ is a polished and confident speaker
- ❖ habla con seguridad y propiedad

- ◆ makes effective demonstrations
- ❖ hace demostraciones eficaces

- ◆ effectively uses an extensive vocabulary
- ❖ usa con eficacia un vocabulario amplio

- ◆ is highly articulate
- ❖ se expresa muy bien

- ◆ makes persuasive presentations
- ❖ hace presentaciones persuasivos

Making Progress (Está Progresando)

- ◆ is beginning to listen consistently
- ❖ comienza a escuchar consistentemente

- ◆ is now communicating with ease
- ❖ ahora se comunica con facilidad

Communication

Making Progress (Está Progresando) *(cont.)*

- ◆ his/her language is more relevant and meaningful
- ❖ su lenguaje es más adecuado y coherente

- ◆ expresses ideas more clearly
- ❖ expresa ideas con más claridad

- ◆ his/her questions are more pertinent
- ❖ sus preguntas son más adecuadas

- ◆ is displaying more self-confidence when speaking
- ❖ demuestra más seguridad en sí mismo(a) cuando habla

- ◆ uses an increasing vocabulary
- ❖ usa un vocabulario más amplio

Needs Improvement (Necesita Mejorar)

- ◆ responds slowly to oral and written directions
- ❖ responde lentamente a instrucciones orales y escritas

- ◆ needs to develop a stronger vocabulary
- ❖ necesita ampliar su vocabulario

- ◆ needs to communicate with confidence
- ❖ necesita comunicarse con más seguridad

- ◆ needs to use concise and clear language
- ❖ necesita usar un lenguaje más conciso y claro

- ◆ needs to state position clearly
- ❖ necesita expresar su postura con claridad

- ◆ needs to develop better listening skills
- ❖ necesita mejorar sus destrezas para escuchar

- ◆ should seek out more opportunities for public speaking
- ❖ debería buscar más oportunidades para hablar en público

Attitude

Proficient (Competente)

◆ has a positive attitude towards school

❖ tiene una actitud positiva hacia la escuela

◆ shows genuine interest in _____

❖ muestra un genuino interés en _____

◆ is eager to participate in _____

❖ se interesa por participar en _____

◆ explores new opportunities

❖ explora nuevas oportunidades

◆ is eager to try new approaches

❖ se interesa en nuevos enfoques

◆ effectively applies new concepts and techniques

❖ aplica con eficacia nuevos conceptos y técnicas

◆ has incredible energy and enthusiasm

❖ tiene una increíble energía y entusiasmo

◆ displays multifaceted vision

❖ demuestra tener una perspectiva polifacética

◆ focuses on the future

❖ se concentra en el futuro

Making Progress (Está Progresando)

◆ is showing an improved attitude

❖ ahora muestra una mejor actitud

◆ his/her improved report card reflects his/her attitude toward school

❖ una mejor boleta de calificaciones refleja su actitud hacia la escuela

◆ displaying more self-confidence

❖ ahora muestra más seguridad en sí mismo(a)

Attitude

Making Progress (Está Progresando) *(cont.)*

- ◆ is showing more interest in _____
- ❖ muestra más interés en _____

- ◆ now sees the connection between learning and his/her future
- ❖ ahora ve la relación entre el aprendizaje y su futuro

- ◆ is exhibiting more initiative
- ❖ muestra más iniciativa

- ◆ has greatly improved level of participation
- ❖ mejoró mucho su nivel de participación

Needs Improvement (Necesita Mejorar)

- ◆ responds slowly
- ❖ responde lentamente

- ◆ needs to improve attitude
- ❖ necesita mejorar su actitud

- ◆ lacks self-confidence
- ❖ carece de seguridad en sí mismo(a)

- ◆ would benefit from trying new approaches
- ❖ se beneficiaría si probara nuevos enfoques

- ◆ needs to direct incredible energy toward learning
- ❖ necesita dedicar mucha energía al aprendizaje

- ◆ needs to seize opportunities to participate
- ❖ necesita aprovechar las oportunidades para participar

- ◆ needs to show more interest in _____
- ❖ necesita mostrar más interés en _____

Creativity

Proficient (Competente)

◆ displays creative imagination

❖ demuestra una imaginación creativa

◆ excels in creative thinking and problem solving

❖ se destaca en el pensamiento creativo y la resolución de problemas

◆ successfully develops creative strategies

❖ desarrolla estrategias creativas con éxito

◆ is very creative

❖ es muy creativo(a)

◆ demonstrates a high degree of originality

❖ demuestra un alto grado de originalidad

◆ possesses many talents and capabilities

❖ tiene muchos talentos y habilidades

◆ possesses a unique combination of skill and talent

❖ tiene una singular combinación de destreza y talento

◆ extremely versatile

❖ muy versátil

Making Progress (Está Progresando)

◆ has started thinking "outside the box"

❖ comienza a tener ideas originales

◆ is beginning to seek creative alternatives

❖ comienza a buscar alternativas creativas

◆ is beginning to use imagination to solve problems

❖ comienza a usar la imaginación para resolver problemas

◆ is becoming aware of hidden talents

❖ comienza a descubrir sus talentos ocultos

Creativity

Making Progress (Está Progresando) *(cont.)*

◆ is showing more originality and creativity

❖ muestra más originalidad y creatividad

◆ now initiates fresh ideas

❖ ahora tiene ideas novedosas

◆ is willing to take more risks

❖ muestra disposición para asumir riesgos

◆ is beginning to nurture his/her curiosity

❖ comienza a alimentar su curiosidad

Needs Improvement (Necesita Mejorar)

◆ encourage _____ to take risks and explore new ideas

❖ motiven a _____ para que asuma más riesgos y explore nuevas ideas

◆ encourage him/her to explore new paths and procedures

❖ motívenlo(a) para que explore nuevos métodos y procedimientos

◆ needs to direct considerable energy to creatively solving problems

❖ necesita dedicar considerable energía a la resolución creativa de problemas

◆ needs guidance to effectively use creative talents

❖ necesita orientación para usar con eficacia sus talentos creativos

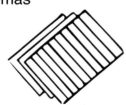

◆ would benefit from lessons to develop creative ability

❖ se beneficiaría si tomara lecciones para desarrollar la creatividad

◆ active imagination needs guidance

❖ imaginación activa que necesita orientación

◆ has the ability to be original

❖ tiene la capacidad de ser original

◆ high degree of creativity not being realized

❖ alto grado de creatividad no aprovechada

Two-Word Phrases

- ◆ challenging problems
- ❖ problemas desafiantes

- ◆ basic strengths
- ❖ fortalezas básicas

- ◆ achieving excellence
- ❖ lograr la excelencia

- ◆ accepting responsibility
- ❖ aceptar la responsabilidad

- ◆ accomplishing results
- ❖ lograr resultados

- ◆ achievement-oriented
- ❖ persigue logros

- ◆ analytical reasoning
- ❖ razonamiento analítico

- ◆ clear expectations
- ❖ expectativas claras

- ◆ competent performer
- ❖ de rendimiento aceptable

- ◆ confident speaker
- ❖ habla en público con seguridad

- ◆ creative solutions
- ❖ soluciones creativas

- ◆ creative strengths
- ❖ fortalezas creativas

- ◆ developing solutions
- ❖ desarrollar soluciones

- ◆ driving force
- ❖ fuerza impulsora

- ◆ dynamic impressions
- ❖ impresiones dinámicas

- ◆ efficient manner
- ❖ con eficiencia

- ◆ enthusiastic spirit
- ❖ espíritu entusiasta

- ◆ exciting challenge
- ❖ desafío motivador

- ◆ extremely resourceful
- ❖ muy hábil

- ◆ favorable impressions
- ❖ impresiones favorables

- ◆ fresh enthusiasm
- ❖ entusiasmo renovado

- ◆ genuine interest
- ❖ interés genuino

- ◆ goal seeker
- ❖ persigue metas

- ◆ high achiever
- ❖ logra grandes metas

- ◆ high potential
- ❖ excelentes aptitudes

- ◆ highly articulate
- ❖ se expresa muy bien

- ◆ highly committed
- ❖ muy dedicado(a)

- ◆ highly competent
- ❖ muy competente

- ◆ highly energized
- ❖ tiene mucha energía

- ◆ imaginative thinking
- ❖ pensamiento imaginativo

Two-Word Phrases

- important contributor
- colaborador(a) importante

- impressive results
- resultados asombrosos

- independent decisions
- decisiones propias

- inner drive
- motivación propia

- innovative thinking
- pensamiento innovador

- intense desire
- deseo intenso

- leadership qualities
- aptitudes de liderazgo

- learning opportunities
- oportunidades de aprender

- maximum effort
- máximo esfuerzo

- measurable results
- resultados medibles

- mental toughness
- tenacidad mental

- new approaches
- nuevos enfoques

- open-minded
- de mente abierta

- optimal results
- resultados óptimos

- peak efficiency
- eficiencia máxima

- personal integrity
- integridad personal

- pleasing personality
- personalidad agradable

- positive attitude
- actitud positiva

- practical thinking
- pensamiento práctico

- proven performer
- de rendimiento probado

- self-starter
- con iniciativa

- solid achiever
- logra sus metas

- strong effort
- gran esfuerzo

- success-oriented
- persigue el éxito

- team motivator
- motivador(a) de equipos

- unique solutions
- soluciones singulares

- visionary thinker
- pensador(a) visionario(a)

- works effectively
- trabaja con eficacia

Helpful Adjectives

- ◆ abundant
- ❖ abundante

- ◆ active
- ❖ activo(a)

- ◆ adept
- ❖ hábil

- ◆ alert
- ❖ alerta

- ◆ ambitious
- ❖ ambicioso(a)

- ◆ articulate
- ❖ se expresa muy bien

- ◆ calm
- ❖ tranquilo(a)

- ◆ capable
- ❖ capaz

- ◆ challenging
- ❖ desafiante

- ◆ compelling
- ❖ convincente

- ◆ competent
- ❖ competente

- ◆ confident
- ❖ seguro(a)

- ◆ courteous
- ❖ cortés

- ◆ curious
- ❖ curioso(a)

- ◆ dedicated
- ❖ dedicado(a)

- ◆ dependable
- ❖ digno(a) de confianza

- ◆ diligent
- ❖ cumplidor(a)

- ◆ distinctive
- ❖ distintivo(a)

- ◆ dynamic
- ❖ dinámico(a)

- ◆ efficient
- ❖ eficiente

- ◆ energetic
- ❖ lleno(a) de energía

- ◆ enthusiastic
- ❖ entusiasta

- ◆ exceptional
- ❖ excepcional

- ◆ extraordinary
- ❖ extraordinario(a)

- ◆ fair
- ❖ justo(a)

- ◆ fine
- ❖ bueno

- ◆ forceful
- ❖ contundente

- ◆ genuine
- ❖ genuino(a)

- ◆ great
- ❖ magnífico(a)

- ◆ helpful
- ❖ colaborador(a)

- ◆ honest
- ❖ honesto(a)

- ◆ imaginative
- ❖ imaginativo(a)

- ◆ independent
- ❖ independiente

- ◆ industrious
- ❖ aplicado(a)

- ◆ innovative
- ❖ innovador(a)

- ◆ knowledgeable
- ❖ informado(a)

- ◆ logical
- ❖ lógico(a)

- ◆ loyal
- ❖ leal

- ◆ magnificent
- ❖ espléndido(a)

- ◆ mature
- ❖ maduro(a)

- ◆ motivated
- ❖ motivado(a)

- ◆ observant
- ❖ observador(a)

Helpful Adjectives

- optimistic
- optimista

- organized
- organizado(a)

- original
- original

- outstanding
- sobresaliente

- perceptive
- perceptivo(a)

- persuasive
- convincente

- pleasant
- agradable

- positive
- positivo(a)

- productive
- productivo(a)

- punctual
- puntual

- realistic
- realista

- remarkable
- notable

- resourceful
- hábil

- respectful
- respetuoso(a)

- self-confident
- seguro de sí mismo(a)

- significant
- significativo(a)

- splendid
- espléndido(a)

- stimulating
- estimulante

- strong
- sólido(a)

- successful
- exitoso(a)

- superb
- magnífico(a)

- superior
- sobresaliente

- supportive
- solidario(a)

- tactful
- diplomático(a)

- thorough
- minucioso(a)

- trustworthy
- fiable

- ultimate
- máximo(a)

- understanding
- comprensivo(a)

- unique
- singular

- unusual
- inusual

- versatile
- versátil

- vibrant
- vibrante

- vigorous
- vigoroso(a)

- well-liked
- popular

- winning (personality)
- encantador(a)

- zestful
- lleno(a) de energía

Helpful Verbs

- accelerates
- acelera

- accepts
- acepta

- accomplishes
- consigue

- achieves
- logra

- acquires
- adquiere

- adapts
- se adapta

- addresses
- se dirige a

- adjusts
- se ajusta

- analyzes
- analiza

- anticipates
- anticipa

- applies
- aplica

- articulates
- articula

- ascertains
- determina

- aspires
- aspira

- asserts
- afirma

- assumes
- asume

- attempts
- intenta

- augments
- aumenta

- broadens
- amplía

- builds
- forja

- calculates
- calcula

- capitalizes
- capitaliza

- challenges
- desafía

- clarifies
- clarifica

- collaborates
- colabora

- communicates
- comunica

- completes
- hace

- comprehends
- comprende

- computes
- calcula

- concentrates
- se concentra

- concludes
- saca conclusiones

- considers
- considera

- contemplates
- contempla

- controls
- controla

- cooperates
- colabora

- creates
- crea

- defines
- define

- delivers
- entrega

- demonstrates
- demuestra

- deserves
- merece

- designs
- diseña

- develops
- desarrolla

- discovers
- descubre

- displays
- exhibe

- earns
- logra

- emphasizes
- subraya

- empowers
- confiere

- encourages
- motiva

- energizes
- da energía

- excels
- se destaca

- extends
- extiende

- facilitates
- facilita

- follows-up
- hace un seguimiento

- foresees
- prevé

- formulates
- formula

- fulfills
- cumple

- gains
- gana

- grasps
- capta

- generates
- genera

- identifies
- identifica

Helpful Verbs

- impacts
- impacta

- implements
- implementa

- impresses
- asombra

- improves
- mejora

- increases
- aumenta

- informs
- informa

- inspires
- inspira

- instructs
  da instrucciones

- integrates
- integra

- interacts
- se relaciona

- interprets
- interpreta

- introduces
- introduce

- investigates
- investiga

- knows
- conoce

- launches
- lanza

- leads
- dirige

- learns
- aprende

- maintains
- mantiene

- maximizes
- maximiza

- modifies
- modifica

- motivates
- motiva

- necessitates
- necesita

- notifies
- notifica

- observes
- observa

- obtains
- obtiene

- operates
- opera

- organizes
- organiza

- overcomes
- supera

- participates
- participa

- possesses
- posee

- practices
- practica

- prioritizes
- da prioridad

- projects
- proyecta

- provides
- da

- realizes
- logra

- recalls
- recuerda

- recognizes
- reconoce

- recommends
- recomienda

- records
- registra

- reflects
- refleja

- reinforces
- refuerza

- represents
- representa

- requires
- requiere

- resolves
- resuelve

- reviews
- revisa

- seeks
- busca

- simplifies
- simplifica

- solves
- soluciona

- strengthens
- refuerza

- strives
- se esmera

- suggests
- sugiere

- supports
- apoya

- surpasses
- supera

- sustains
- sostiene

- thinks
- piensa

- understands
- entiende

- unifies
- unifica

- utilizes
- usa

- verifies
- verifica

- weighs
- compara